\ | /
25 Brilliant Speakers
Their Expert Advice to Springboard Your Speaking Career

Also from Splendor Publishing

The Art & Science of Loving Yourself First
'cause Your Business Should Complete You,
Not Deplete You!

Positive x Positive = Unlimited
High Octane Positive Energy

Start Right Marketing
The Business of Making an Impact

Winning Ways in Commercial Real Estate
18 Successful Women Unveil the Tips of the Trade
in the Real Estate World

The Happy Law Practice
Expert Strategies to Build Business While
Maintaining Peace of Mind

The Influential Entrepreneur:
Position Yourself for Win-Win Engagement

25 Brilliant Business Mentors
Their Top Tips to Catapult You to Success

Accessorizing for Design Professionals
A Guide for Interior Designers, Decorators, and
Color Consultants

The Substance of Faith
Get Hooked—It's Good Stuff!

\ l /
25 Brilliant Speakers
Their Expert Advice to Springboard Your Speaking Career

Co-authored by

Margo DeGange `\l/` Timothy Grant Carter `\l/` Forbes Riley

Jim Ross Meskimen `\l/` Carla Ferrer `\l/` Tracy Repchuk

Caterina Rando `\l/` Debbie Saviano `\l/` Tonya Hofmann

Fantastic Frank Johnson `\l/` Candy Barone `\l/` Fred Schuldt

Elayna Fernández `\l/` Ha Tran `\l/` Susan Tolles

Gabrielle Smith `\l/` Elisha `\l/` Elyssa `\l/` Kimberly Pitts

Kathy Kingston `\l/` Liz Uram `\l/` Elizabeth Quintanilla

Bruce Keith `\l/` Shirley Dalton `\l/` Clarissa Gatdula-Calingasan

Compiled and Edited by

Margo DeGange, M.Ed.

Splendor Publishing
College Station, TX

SPLENDOR PUBLISHING
Published by Splendor Publishing
College Station, TX.

First published printing, November 2014

Library of Congress Control Number: 2014921526
25 Brilliant Speakers
Their Expert Advice to Springboard Your Speaking Career
1. Business 2. Marketing

ISBN-10: 1-940278-20-1
ISBN-13: 978-1-940278-20-9

Business/Marketing
Printed in the United States of America.

Artwork: Igor Sokalski | 23373731 | Dreamstime.com

For more information or to order bulk copies of this book for events,
seminars, conferences, or training, please contact
SplendorPublishing.com.

Dedication

This book is dedicated to the leaders, speakers, entrepreneurs, and individuals with purposeful and meaningful life-work, who understand the importance of their message and mission. My hope and prayer is that the words within the pages of this book will motivate, inspire, and equip you to bring your life-giving work to others through the miracle of the speaking platform. My hat is off to you, my hands applaud you, and my heart is for you. Make your speeches memorable and your every word count for yourself and others!

⋛Contents⋚

⋛Introduction⋜

There's a small, courageous group on the face of planet Earth called "speakers." You may know one, or you may be one! These people are passionate and brave, and almost always have a vision for what they think the future could be, even if just for a tiny community, niche, or segment of the world.

Speakers come in a variety of interesting shapes, sizes, and colors. There's a brilliant one out there for every event need.

Yet how . . . how do they become brilliant? As well, how do they *stay* brilliant? Do they go to Brilliant Speaker's School? Do they take a break on occasion from professional speaking to earn CEU credits to keep their Brilliant Speaker status?

We both know the answers to those silly questions. What we may not know is what a brilliant speaker does day by day to become brilliant, to be brilliant, and to stay brilliant. Wouldn't you love to be privy to that insider information? Well the news today is wonderful . . . with this book in hand, you can!

In this gem of a book for up and coming speakers (seasoned speakers, too), twenty-five brilliant and experienced mentors gather with top-notch information to help you catapult your speaking career quickly and with ease. You get actionable insider-tips and strategies from some of the most sought-after and impressive stage personalities in a variety of fields, so you can succeed beyond your wildest speaking aspirations!

These mentors include all kinds of people, from celebrities and show hosts, to survivors, community leaders, and mom-bloggers! Most importantly, they are people just like you, who started out unsure and not knowing what to do, yet forged ahead with a desire and determination to make a significant impact in the lives of others through speaking.

These are class act people, like Fantastic Frank Johnson, who ditched the body bag in exchange for life, and Jim Ross Meskimen, the personable and intelligent son of Happy Day's mom Marion Ross, who created his own identity as a popular impressionist, comedian, and voice artist. Then there's Tracy Repchuk, a once-upon-a-time, behind-the-scenes software creator who now speaks internationally, encouraging regular folks like us to use the Internet to spread their messages. Forbes Riley has something to share, too, about being true to who you are; she should know, she transformed her health and her career, and used the spotlight to sell millions in products and change lives worldwide.

Add to this list *all* of the other amazing speakers in this book, including two successful pre-teen entrepreneurs; a world-class body-builder; a social media butterfly; a fiery, faith-filled outdoorsman; a two-time cancer survivor (two of them, actually); a beautiful model who transformed her looks and career from ordinary to extraordinary; a gracious and passionate mentor for women across the globe; a leader of a world-class organization for speakers; a leader of a world-class organization for women; a global publisher; a tell-it-like-it-is powerhouse change-agent; an inspired leadership guru; a leadership master of hope; a fire-ball vegan mompreneur; a visionary who embraced her own power before positively changing hundreds of lives; a branding expert who attracts people effortlessly with her authentic, personal style; a passionate real estate coach who models super success for his clients; an engineer who breaks down the complex and makes it easy to see the big opportunities; a couple of shining, radio superstars; a pre-eminent multi-million dollar fundraising expert who once sold a tangerine for thousands; and an only child of taxi proprietors, who honked at defeat and pain, and accelerated her business to success!

Introduction

These incredible speakers are down-to-earth, caring, simple people like most of us are, yet they defeated the odds that pretended to be against them. Now they are showing up candidly for you, bright-eyed, and telling no tales, to help you succeed from the stage.

This diverse group of stage-mentors may seem very different, but they actually share common thoughts and knowledge in some respects. As you dive into this book, you will gain advice from all of them, and you will soon see that many of them touch on some of the same topics, but give a unique viewpoint when they do. This was my intention.

When I asked the writers to be a part of this project, none of them knew what the others would write about. I gave each one the same list of more than fifty topics, and I wanted every co-author to be free to share on the topics they felt compelled to address. Having insight into their various "takes" is a grand part of this work. It allows you to compare and contrast, and reminds you not to get stuck—that there's rarely ever just one way of doing a thing! It compels you to stay open.

Among the writers, you will see recurring themes, like be yourself, use humor with finesse, ignore the naysayers, tell your stories, but there are hundreds of one-of-a-kind nuggets, too.

None of the authors saw the manuscript or the writing of their co-authors until the book was published. That way no one could change their focus. I like that about this work! I like it a lot! I love that this book is organic: that I did not script what the co-authors should share.

You will see the value in it, too, once you start reading and get into the mindsets of the different authors. Some have been speaking for many years, and some are newer to the scene, but all are intent on their mission, focused on their purpose, on-point with their goals, and successful in their lives. They were chosen because of that, with you in mind.

So much goes into developing a strong speaking career and building your skill-set for the stage. You'll need to know how to competently and proficiently do things like overcome fear, understand audience needs, strategically use humor, increase your confidence and perceived value, market your speaking services, use social media to advance, brand for growth, engage with your audience, create influential relationships, host your own events, craft and tell your story, and plenty more. There's much to master. Who can show you how?

We can! In this book you will experience insights from a plethora of successful speakers of various backgrounds and mindsets; some are faith-based in their work; some are focused on the bottom line of revenues, some have been through tragedy; and some have tried many things until they finally found what worked. No matter: each and every one of them has tremendous value in what they know, have experienced, and now share with you.

And here it is! *25 Brilliant Speakers: Their Expert Advice to Springboard your Speaking Career*. Put away your phone. Grab your favorite beverage. Get cozy and comfy. Have an "Aha Sheet" and pen ready so you can jot down those mega brain bursts! Have a "Take-Action Sheet" ready, too. Then, get busy learning to be the next brilliant speaker in your field.

This book is a labor of love, designed with one clear goal: to help you springboard your speaking career quickly and with ease, so you can fulfill your calling with confidence. You most definitely can become a brilliant speaker! We think the advice within these pages will set the stage and pull back the curtain for your ongoing and continual success.

To Your Brilliant Speaking Career,

Margo DeGange

1

≥Brilliant Advice≤
from Margo DeGange

A Super Model for Speakers

She's gorgeous! She's stunning! She is rare indeed! She is like nothing I have ever seen! Of course she is—she's the super model for speakers, and I want you to gawk and stare at her intently for the next several pages!

In presenting the opening chapter in a book by speakers for speakers, it seems especially fitting to lay the foundation with a model that will help us understand the big, at-a glance picture of our role as speakers, and that of the audience.

I'd like to share with you an instructional design model I created that can substantially help you in your speaking career as well as in your business in general.

It might help pave the way if you know just a little bit about me and where I am coming from in writing this *super model* chapter for you. My college undergraduate work was in leadership and communication, with a focus area in business and economics. My master's education was in *adult learning* and *adult motivation.* I have been formally trained as an *adult education expert* and a *professional instructional designer*. This training—with all the research and case studies I have done—comes in handy each and every day as a *Business & Lifestyle Designer*!

Several years ago (about fifteen), I created a visual model for speakers, facilitators, and trainers which I formally named, *Audience-Centered Instructional Design Components*. In more recent years, I informally re-named it, *Margo's Model*. To some, the formal name may sound a little boring, hence the informal name, *Margo's Model* (and if you know me well, as some of my readers and clients do, you know I am anything but boring). In reality, my audience model is quite enlightening, and wildly exciting, yet it is timeless and reliably solid.

The model was meant to help speakers and trainers who create and deliver content, which most all of us speakers do. The exciting part though, is that the model is a highly useful tool that provides us with a beautiful way to understand and connect with our audience (and our clients, too).

Right here, I'm going to break it down for you, and play with it, so you can fully monetize what you learn from this cool little model, known on the streets as *Margo's Model*.

The model consists of nine important components that should always be included in the design of good instruction, as well as in the delivery. Eight of them circle around the CORE component, which is the most vital of all—the audience. Of the eight surrounding components, there's no particular order of importance; they are of equal importance and they all need to be considered in every speech you design and deliver.

The audience RULES . . . sorry, *you don't!* Everything we do in our speaking businesses must be to connect to and relate well with the audience, so that we create shared meaning (the goal of communication) and a mutually beneficial relationship; one that results in audience members taking positive action and you getting invited back to speak and help change lives.

On the following page you can see the model at-a-glance. Look at this *super model* lovingly and with true desire as we go through the eight components surrounding your audience.

Audience-Centered Instructional Design Components
a.k.a.
Margo's Model

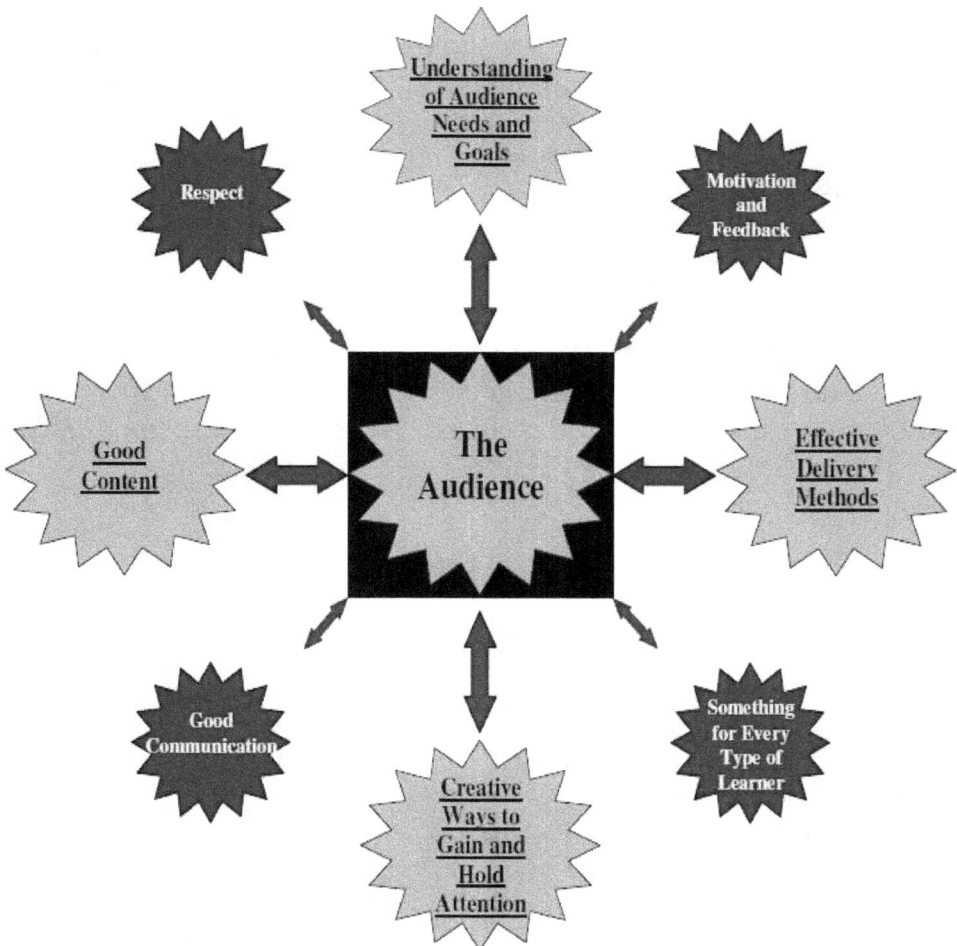

Understanding of Audience Needs and Goals

Respect

Motivation and Feedback

Good Content

The Audience

Effective Delivery Methods

Good Communication

Creative Ways to Gain and Hold Attention

Something for Every Type of Learner

MargoDeGange.com

Component 1:
Understanding of Audience Needs and Goals

It's *our* responsibility to discover what our audience needs, not what we *think* they need. Know the goals of your audience, and why they need your help to meet these important goals.

Some speakers spend a lot of time focusing on what they do, and crafting a niche that sets them apart. That's fine, but what's not fine is overly focusing on that at the expense of keeping a solid focus on what you do for the audience member.

Always keep your main focus on how you affect lives for the better. Your information, content, ability to persuade, motivational strategy—in general, your talks—should be more about what you do for them than what you do!

Be so geared in that direction, that when someone asks, "*What do you do?*" you easily respond with the desired results you help people gain. If you're super focused on understanding and knowing the needs and goals of your audience, it will roll off your tongue when you're asked, "*What do you speak on?*"

⩒ *Brilliant Quick Tip* ⩐

When ask what you speak on, be ready to tell the desired results you provide!

Component 2:
Motivation and Feedback

When we communicate, we have to trigger something in our audience that will cause them to want to interact back—in some way—giving us vital information and stirring up in themselves the intrinsic motivation to make needed change. Motivation also involves you—the speaker—using specific strategies to keep the audience intrigued. Their feedback means they feel free to respond because we are open to them, or because we listen and also offer feedback.

Component 3:
Effective Delivery Methods

Methods matter! Delivery methods involve how information is presented to learners, such as through webinars, seminars, books, the stage, etc. The methods you use to communicate should be effective, because they ultimately affect results.

Delivery methods—I believe—are not limited to the delivery channels we use (Internet, stage, etc.). There are methods of delivery closer to home that communicate how much you care.

What message does your demeanor, your dress, your overall presence, your facial expressions, your clarity, your tempo, your main points, your body language, your props, your tone of voice, your attitude, your interactivities, your gestures, your jokes, your degree of support and engagement, your stories, your transitions, and the environment, deliver to the audience?

What about the methods that communicate our message and care even before we are selected for a specific stage? What does your media kit say about you? How about your website, your voicemail, your office, your receptionist, your team, your social media stream, your speaker's sheet, your book, your emails, your bio, and your one-sheet? Are they *effective* in supporting the brand "mood and personality" you want to promote?

Then consider the messages that "other methods" might deliver on your behalf: your level of cooperation with meeting planners, your need to be a diva or to be "right," and even your car (is it obnoxiously loud pulling up—in need of a tune-up?).

> ⋛ *Brilliant Quick Tip* ⋚
>
> *Methods of delivery aren't limited to books,
> seminars, the Internet, etc. They include all
> things about you that send a message. You
> are what you say, do, wear, and allow.*

Component 4:
Something for Every Type of Learner

This is self-explanatory. Not every audience member will relate equally well to the same techniques you use to get your message across, and although we're all quite capable of learning from various modes and cues (visual, auditory, or kinesthetic), most people have a strong *preference mode* of learning (you often hear, "*I'm a visual learner*").

Did you know that almost seven out of every ten people in most age brackets prefer visual learning cues (sixty-five percent of us, according to the Social Science Research Network). Yet many speakers never unveil a prop or pull a rabbit out of their hat! Even if you do, you still must not forget the thirty to thirty-five percent of people who prefer to learn by touch and sound.

So, mate, mix it up! Offer a variety of engagement tools—bells, whistles, and gentle thistles if you will—to easily appeal to the many different preferences of your audience.

Component 5:
Creative Ways to Gain and Hold Attention

Be innovative and creative. Have fun with it, and get people talking. Give your audience a super-simple task to do; offer them a sliver of insider info they otherwise would never be privy to; facilitate a meaningful, hands-on interactivity if the environment and set-up allow; demonstrate an important principle through movement or visuals; play a song or whistle a quick tune. Be a super-cool presenter, not a talking meatball (see, I could have just said "talking head").

Gain and hold the attention of your beloved audience with new ideas, new considerations, new concepts, and rich content that matters deeply to them. Don't overdo it, just ***do it*** well!

Component 6:
Good Communication

What the world needs now, is love, sweet love*. . . are you singing the song now? These lyrics help me address two crucial points for speakers: 1) have a heart of love, and sincerely care about your audience so you stand (no pun or cliché intended) to communicate well, and 2) don't use cliché's of any sort in your speeches—they bore me . . . and they bore you, too, and oh *YES*, they also grossly bore the audience.

Communication that flows well and which feels natural, positive, clear, and simple, actually takes great planning and effort on the part of the speaker. You must edit out all of the unnecessary and ambiguous content, and stick like a wet spring roll wrap to your main idea and the key points that support it.

As I mentioned previously, the goal of communication is to "create shared meaning." Let your audience identify with the very values you came to amplify. Reiterate through your speech the intimate understanding that you are in this together, and that together, you are solving a problem or finding a better solution than the one that was there before.

"What the World Needs Now is Love,"1965, lyrics by Hal David, music by Burt Bacharach.

Indulge your audience in the knowledge and experience of what it is like for the two of you to *create shared meaning*.

Communication goes both ways, so be sure to "hear," notice, and respond to what the audience is "saying" to you as well.

Component 7:
Good Content

If your content is junk, no one will care and everyone will waste their time and resources. Research your topic well; gather lots of quality information that takes you some digging to get to. Then, edit it down to a clean plate of exquisitely desirable goodies, the way a skilled chef infuses a dish with various—and sometimes unusual—flavors, and then presents it in beautiful fashion to the eagerly awaiting dinner guest.

Good content is always tied to desirable results, and great speakers always consider **outcomes**. They don't speak to hear themselves perform; they speak to get results. Ask the decision-maker who hired you to speak, what they desire as an outcome. In other words, what results do they want for their group? What behavior change would they like to see once you have spoken and left? Don't assume you know the desired outcome; ask! Then use this information to craft your speech.

Many inexperienced speakers yuck up their speeches with too many goodies. For every speech you create, be it a keynote, after dinner speech, breakout session, or general session, choose just one major outcome and focus your content on delivering for that outcome.

With your outcome in mind when preparing your content, have one main message to convey, with *three* of what I call *Key Points of Learning*, or KPL (it's the instructional designer in me). On paper, you can call them bullet points, or the ABC points, but be sure and have them in advance, to guide your speech and to transfer learning. Each KPL should be clearly tied to the main message and help to facilitate the desired outcome you have in mind for your audience.

⋛ *Brilliant Quick Tip* ⋚

For each speech, choose one desired outcome; focus your content on that, with one main message and three Key Points of Learning. That's all!

Component 8:
Respect

All any of us want in this big, wonderful universe is to feel we are seen, heard, and that we matter. That's really *it*! The people I respect most are those who make the effort to "see" me and acknowledge my value. If you know your audience is as valuable as you, and their lives just as important to them as yours is to you, you'll be batting a zillion (bet you thought I'd write "a thousand"). Braid that with genuine care for others, and you have a chord that can't be broken; it's called "respect"!

This *Audience-Centered Instructional Design Components*, model, a.k.a., *Margo's Model* will never be outdated or old news, because people will always want to be validated, seen, and understood. If, with every speech you give, you can focus on that inner CORE component, which is your audience, and create and deliver your speeches with the surrounding eight components top-of-mind and relating to that inner core, you will absolutely be a brilliant and wildly successful speaker!

About Margo DeGange

Margo DeGange, M.Ed, international best-selling author, speaker, and non-fiction book publisher, is an adult learning and adult motivation expert, a business mentor, and a lifestyle designer. Margo has a solid and proven track record for showing clients worldwide how to grow their client base, expand their influence, increase their income, improve their relationships and communication, and significantly enrich their lives through the *power of words* and with meaningful, content marketing and content publishing.

Her in-demand, inspirational, and life-changing training, consulting, and speeches began in the interior design, training, and speaking fields, and quickly grew from there. She has spoken at important live events and gatherings from coast to coast and internationally. For more than twenty-five years, Margo has helped entrepreneurs and individuals get their messages out so they can communicate to connect with others.

Margo is the founder of Women of Splendor, the exciting faith-based organization where spiritually-minded women with important life-work collaborate, get mentored, develop their "Gift of Brilliance," increase their reach, visibility, and discoverability, and bring healing to the world in a BIG and splendid way! She is also the founder of Splendor Publishing.

Learn more about Margo DeGange at:
MargoDeGange.com

2

≳Brilliant Advice≲
from Timothy Grant Carter, a.k.a. "Slam"

11 Surefire Tips to Jump-Start Your Speaking Career

In this chapter, you will learn eleven powerful techniques to help you develop your speaking abilities and hone your skills to become an effective, dynamic speaker. Implementing these tips will help you reach audiences convincingly. Utilizing them will give you the power to produce significant results and inspire positive change in your listeners.

Technique #1: *Have a Clear Focus for Your Talk*

What is your purpose? How do you want your audience to think, feel, and act after you finish?

To be a powerful speaker, you must have a compelling and laser-focused purpose for your message. Everything in your talk must *drive* towards this purpose! A good public speaker is deeply passionate about their purpose, and the point of their talk is clear; it reaches out and "grabs" the audience.

A good speaker must focus on the outcome, stay connected, and make sure the audience is engaged during delivery. It is impossible to obtain maximum results with your listeners if you are not on target.

I will give two examples to explain this idea. First, let's think of a popular recreational pursuit for comparison: laser-tag and paintball. The only way to win is to aim well and clearly hit your targets. It is very plain if you hit your targets, and hitting the targets is the only way to win the game. Focus your laser on winning the audience over to your point. Put the paint color on them and clearly hit your mark . . . persuade them!

Here is another illustration, for outdoorsmen like me. You can think of your speech as being similar to a rabbit hunt. You know the rabbit will move but you train to move with him. Your hunt chases the rabbit, wherever he goes. If the rabbit moves into the bushes, so must you. You must keep your mind on the rabbit and not be distracted by other things. You must keep your focus on him to be successful in your hunt. The point of your speaking is like pursuing the rabbit. Everything must drive towards this point.

To effectively communicate with your listeners, you must align with them. Do not leave them behind. Connect with your audience on a deep level. Let your passion lead the way and make it easier for them to emotionally connect with you.

Drive your point . . . passionately pursue your topic. Work everything you say towards your call for commitment. Be fervent, consistent, and patiently relentless about the goal of your speech. Let your listeners sense that you are on a passionate mission—for *their* good.

Make every illustration, every example, every humorous anecdote, and every point you deliver be directed towards the purpose of your talk. Be totally purposeful. Be driven.

Utilize the "you" factor to get it across. "Wow" the people with your commitment to the aim and direction of the speech. Use every means to connect with them *and* to connect them with your point. Draw them, coax them, entertain them, and humor them. Lead them with every tool in your speaker's tool chest toward the conclusion you want to communicate.

Let the conclusion be so strong that they reach the verdict and intended outcome. Let the major point of your message be so clear it is the inescapable conclusion your listener must reach when hearing your talk.

⋨ *Brilliant Quick Tip* ⋩

Make every illustration, every example, every humorous anecdote, and every point you deliver be directed towards the purpose of your talk.

What all this means first and foremost in this: *you must be completely sold on the focus of your message. You must stay on track delivering your talk. You must be abundantly clear about your target!*

Put your laser on showing your point to the audience. Keep the colorful paint of your aim on this target. Have a driving sense of purpose! Remember Tip #1: to be a powerful speaker, you must have a compelling and laser clear purpose for your message. Everything in your talk must be about it!

Technique #2: *Plan Definite Strategies to Overcome Stage Jitters and Unexpected Speaking Difficulties*

Let this be a part of your speaking plan and preparation. One of the most effective ways to overcome nerves before and even during your talk is isometric exercises. These techniques are a great way to diffuse excess energy.

You can press palm against palm to dissipate nerves and jitters. No one will notice and you will definitely feel relief.

There are other isometric tricks—such as foot pressure on the floor and pressing on the podium—that work without drawing attention. These Tricks diffuse nervous pressure effectively and help you relax as you get ready to speak.

Mental tricks also help. Early in life as I was getting ready for an oratorical contest, I will never forget a speaking coach telling me to pretend everyone in the audience was a cabbage head. The comic relief of doing this is considerable. It is almost impossible to be uptight as a speaker when you are talking to a room full of cabbages.

There are other mental approaches to tone down the way you are looking at the audience. The point is to have your own strategies that make you light and loose in your own skin while on the stage. Conversational, comfortable, speakers are much more effective than up-tight and nervy ones.

I have practiced one of these mental approaches for many years in the speaking arena. It is having a mindset of *rigid flexibility*. Don't sweat the small stuff and remember . . . it's all small stuff. Be ready for unexpected changes. Unexpected changes are a part of the speaking pursuit and must be considered normal.

For this reason, always be ready to spontaneously change your speech if you are called on to do so. This flexibility will make you a bigger winner in the speaking arena. Avoiding frustration and finding fulfillment in the role of a public speaker demands that you be flexible. Roll with the punches. Move with the moment like a dancer moves with the music. Be mirthful and relaxed when something unexpected happens.

Practicing these simple strategies of Tip #2 can help you turn jitters and the unexpected into part of your effectiveness as a speaker.

Technique #3: *Power Up Before You Talk*

Warm up for a speech like an athlete warms up to compete. I have a 1977 truck that I love to drive. It is a blast. It performs well, but one thing I always have to remember with my truck is that I must warm it up first. You can't just jump in and take off. It requires some preparation time to be ready to drive.

Speaking effectively is a lot like that. There are specific things you must do to warm yourself up and to do your best work as a speaker. Be solidly ready. Have your content clear and accurate. If you use notes, have them very plain and in big print.

Commit yourself to making a difference with your talk. Develop the internal conviction—before standing before the group—that you will touch them with deep meaning. Gain a faith perspective and belief before you ever start your talk. Believe *before* you begin that you will move your listener's to an important decision.

As a part of your warm up, you may benefit from literally watching yourself in the mirror. Mirror practice can help you see how your facial expressions are likely to be perceived by the audience. Will they see what you want them to see? Mirror practice can answer this question. Try it and see if it helps you. I pray before I talk, always, even if the speech is a secular business presentation. Prayer centers me and helps clarify my motives. It puts my thoughts in order.

Lastly, give yourself a window of final preparation—a final fifteen to thirty minutes alone. At this time, do a sync of your intentions, resources, and content. This is like tuning up a guitar before you play; it clarifies that you are on key. Tip #3 is to power up before you talk. Your messages will be stronger if you do.

Technique #4: *Fill the Room*

Practice being resonant. Work on being clear. Clarify that your volume is sufficient. Never be flat. Fill the room with your energy. Let the people not only hear your talk but feel it in your expressive delivery. Fill the room. It is always a good idea to know the volume required to reach the back row of your audience. No one can benefit if they cannot hear you or if they have to strain to hear what you say.

⋛ *Brilliant Quick Tip* ⋚

Let the people not only hear your talk but "feel" it with your expressive delivery.

Will you use a microphone and amplification? Have you tested this? Let your persona resonate. Have an attitude of humble respect, but a delivery of powerful confidence and conviction. Generate energy in the room. Do not be full of hype, but definitely be on your "A" game with sincere enthusiasm. Nobody likes a "flat" talk.

Let the audience "feel" your words. Don't just say them; artfully convey them. Make each person feel they are the only person in the room. Let it be that you are speaking just to them. Make sure to make eye contact all over the room. Let all listeners know that you are interested in them, because you are!

Being told I "fill the room" is a compliment that I have been told repeatedly. It leads to standing ovations. Let it be said also of you! Tip #4: fill the room.

Technique #5: *Have Original Illustrations*

Think of unexpected ways to get your point across. Have illustrations that are clear and unique to you.

Recently at a meeting, I had a volunteer hand out rocks to audience members before my talk. Then, I used a large rock in my hand during the talk to illustrate my major point. It was *the rock of power*, and yes, you guessed, the rock I gave to them became *their* rock of power. I used this very unusual illustration to gain the commitment of my audience. I used it as a point of reference to keep them on track with my message. In the end, I made it a part of bringing them to the conviction I had been driving at. It was a powerful, original way to make my point.

Bring the audience into your message through original tools you use. Invoke their interest by illustrations that are clearly unique. Help them retain your points by sharing images that will stay in their mind long after your talk is concluded.

Tip #5 is to use original illustrations. This can turn you into a very memorable speaker.

Technique #6: *Insert Humor . . . Use it in Every Talk*

Anyone can learn to use humor. Humor does not always have to be original. You can gain inspiration from other's humor (of course you must make it your own) and have it work well. One important qualifier: test these witticisms on others before you use them behind the lectern.

Sense when your audience is antsy or bored. Change your rhythm. Add variety to the pace, with a joke. Give the people something to laugh at, and then go back to your serious talk. This will create renewed interest and keep the listener on track with you.

While you prepare, make a decision to use humor. Never leave it out. It is like seasoning on a steak. The steak always tastes better when you season it. Your speech will always be received better with a little humor.

Make your humor relevant to the audience. Tie it into your theme. Then, instead of it being a distraction, it will be a part of the goal of your talk. Humor can be an effective part of driving towards a commitment. Tip #6: use humor in your speeches consistently and deliberately.

Technique #7: *Use the Power of Persuasion*

Never forget that you are on a mission of persuasion. Be a master persuader when you take the stage. If you are to make a difference in the minds of your listeners, you must move them with your points. These points generally must be ideas they would not have otherwise thought of themselves. You are the expert; prove it to your audience with powerful, personal examples.

Don't forget to use outside evidence, such as facts gathered from white paper support and professional data. Have proof-texts built into your talk to show the listeners you know what you are talking about. Convince them of the importance and solidity of your message. Tip #7: use the power of persuasion.

Technique #8: *The Drive and the Putt—Start and Finish Strong*

I am not a prolific golfer to say the least. Still, there are aspects of the game that explain key ingredients of making a good speech.

In the game of golf, you must hit the ball hard and straight off the tee, with accuracy. You must drive well. Likewise, in your speaking endeavor, you must begin your talk with a very strong point. This is necessary to gain the interest of your listener and convince them of the importance of your topic. It is critical to start the talk off right.

Thereafter in the game of golf, you must continue good performance on the fairways. This is comparable to the body of your speech, which must follow through on your good start.

After the fairway comes a really critical part in the game; the green. Everything you have gained from the tee and the fairway can be lost here if you are not careful. You must putt with precision. You must finish with finesse.

In the same way, you must finish your talk with great care. Too much—or too little—at this point can ruin the achievement of your whole talk.

To finish, delicately articulate and deliver fine points that artfully craft the *ball* into the *hole*, i.e., the *goal* into the *minds of the listeners*. These finishing points must clearly convey the major message of your speech. These points must hit the flag and score. You must sense the "AHA" moment of the audience when they get it. At this crucial moment, you must deliver neither too much nor too little. Exacting execution is your finale!

Driving introductions start speeches with winning style, while fine-tuned finishes end them that way! In the introduction of your speech, tell them what to expect with confident conviction. Deliver this in detail in the body, with a clear tie to their personal benefit. But in the conclusion, bring it all home; call for action and give them a reason to do it now!

For success, neither part of the game can be overlooked. You must drive hard and follow through well. You must finish carefully, with eagle-eye accuracy and aim. Both are important: to win in the game of golf and in the profession of speaking. Tip #8: start and finish strong!

Technique #9: *Be a Conductor*

Don't just use gestures. Be animated. Be invested in your talk. Let your audience see what you are saying in how you move. Get into it. Let your expressions and gestures exclaim what you are saying with your lips. If you feel it, show your audience with your motions and emotion. Tip #9: be a conductor.

> *⋛ Brilliant Quick Tip ⋜*
>
> *Don't just use gestures. Be animated.*
> *Be invested in your talk.*

Technique #10: *Use Bright, Creative, Vivid, Word Pictures in Your Speaking*

Use illustrations that create visual images in the minds of the listeners. Use your imagination. Be clever. Be colorful. Be clear but expressive.

Entertain your listeners. Let them enjoy listening to you. Practice enhancing your speech with creative expressions, inventive phrases, memorable sayings, and quotations.

Regularly spend time in your dictionary and thesaurus, to increase the visual power of your vocabulary. Making the major points of your talk memorable often involves making them visual.

Use parables. Parables are simple stories that illustrate lessons. Parables, like the master teacher Jesus used, are great ways to make your points stick with your listeners. Share life and cultural events that mean something to you, and relate them to situations that mean something to them!

Utilize proverbs. Use sayings that convey colorful imagery and yet make truth clear. A catchy phrase can be a major key to listeners retaining what you say.

Can you see what you say? This is important. Many of your listeners are visual learners. Are you creating word pictures that convey what you are saying, in visual terms?

In your preparation, practice not only what you say but how you say it. Creating word pictures is an awesome method of insuring successful speaking events and pleased audiences. Tip #10: use bright, creative, vivid word pictures in your speaking.

Technique #11: *Develop a Brand*

There are definite things about you which make you valuable and important as a speaker. I am known as "Slam," and this nickname fits me well. There are many aspects to my life and style that deliver *dynamism* and *help to my listeners*. My performance partner calls these traits "Slamisms."

That is me. That is who I am, and I am comfortable presenting that to others. Yet, I still work on this regularly.

So, work on your public image. What are your unique qualities? What are values and characteristics that define your speaking style? What distinctive traits do you hold that can become your own "brand"? Don't copy anyone else's. Be yourself. But it may take some work to really see your characteristics that are most marketable to others.

"Slam, I am." That is my brand. Even so, work on building and developing your individual "brand" of speaking. Tip #11 reminds you to develop your own brand.

These eleven power tips were designed to help you greatly improve your speaking skills once you have applied them. Now go! Use these them to change the world for good with your powerful, spoken message. You can do it!

About Timothy Grant Carter, a.k.a. "Slam"

Timothy Grant Carter, the positive, fiery, and highly sought-after, inspirational speaker who helps individuals and organizations *"Springboard to Significance,"* is a Career Catalyst and award-winning, multi-million dollar sales professional whose stellar work is recognized and applauded both internationally and in the USA. He is a best-selling author whose wit and keen insights have his readers consistently asking for more. He's the fun creator of the popular blog articles called *"Beams."* Each Beam is captivating, entertaining, and full of useful tips and top-notch information to help entrepreneurs and career professionals own their significance.

Timothy is well-known in business circles as "SLAM," for his no-nonsense approach. A popular and motivating keynote speaker and sales trainer, he knows how to effectively connect with audiences and inspire them for results. He empowers others with original sayings and visionary insight, and his hundreds of speaking engagements include many Christian messages and multitudes of keynotes and sales presentations in the corporate environment.

His best-selling book, *Positive x Positive = Unlimited*, was chosen by editors as an Amazon "Best Books," and his rare business insight was featured in the book, *25 Brilliant Business Mentors*. SLAM knows how to inspire audiences to take action, and individuals to create meaningful and successful lives!

Learn more about at Timothy Grant Carter at:
TimothyGrantCarter.com

3

≩Brilliant Advice≩
from Forbes Riley

Plan Your Message for the Goal in Mind

How does what you say land in the heart of those listening to you? Being mindful of the answer to this question at all times drives the most impactful speakers and has been my personal secret to success.

One of the most important things that I have learned throughout my career and through coaching others is to begin with the end in mind—knowing what you want. When it comes to speaking, understanding how your message is received is the foundation of being able to get what you want when you speak. There's certainly a utility to this; it isn't just raw talent and showmanship, but there are formulas and techniques that can help you get the results you desire, and it's important to break down the parts if you ever want to improve your craft.

There's a parable I often tell about a woodsman and an archer: one day a woodsman was walking through the forest, and he began seeing all of these bull's-eye painted on trees, and one after the other he noticed something extraordinary. Dead center on all of the bull's-eyes were arrows. This archer must be amazing, he thought to himself. After about the fifteenth tree, seeing bull's-eye after bull's-eye with arrows in the center of every one, he was hoping to meet the archer with such skill and flawless precision. Suddenly, he sees a man with a bag of arrows slung over his back and a bow in his hand. "*Excuse me, sir!*" he yelled out, "*Are you responsible for shooting all of these bull's-eyes in these trees?*" "Yes," said the archer half hiding behind a tree in the distance. The woodsman starts approaching him and said, "*You're amazing! I've never seen such marksmanship. Do you think you could show me how you do it?*" "*Well, sure. It's easy,*" said the archer. He steps out from behind the tree and fires an arrow at another tree in the distance, hitting the tree. "All you have to do," he said to the woodsman "*is to shoot the arrow and then paint the bull's eye around it.*"

Begin with the end in mind—know what you want. Do you want to sell a product, sign an investor, cultivate partners, motivate voters, stimulate a movement, or get a job or a marriage proposal? Whatever it is you want—know exactly what that is and then make your plan aimed at achieving that goal. Because one thing I can promise you is that if you don't know exactly what you want, it's not likely you'll ever get it.

> ⋛ *Brilliant Quick Tip* ⋜
>
> *Know exactly what you want and then make your plan aimed at achieving that goal.*

I dedicate an early part of my coaching sessions with each client participating in an intensive soul-searching exercise, having them explore what they want. As a person, and as a professional in life, I ask them: "*What do you want?*" When they finally dig down to the core of their unique answer to this question, the self-revelations are powerful. And it is from these self-revelations that we can begin building the foundation of whatever it is that's needed to get there—to develop the pitch, the performance plan, the platform, the speech, etc.

Conversely, a pitfall to avoid is to *not know what you want* when you speak. If clarity on this issue evades you, begin with deciding what your audience needs. Make key assumptions about who your audience is, and allow those assumptions to drive your plan: what do they value, what do they need from you, what will motivate them to take action, how can you reach in and touch them in a memorable way based on what you know or presume about them? One of the reasons I am successful at what I do is because I don't focus on what I want to say so much as I focus on what my audience needs to hear.

That particular focus amplifies my responsibility as a speaker; I'm not only responsible for what comes out of my mouth, and how, but I'm also responsible for how it's received and how it affects my audience. See the difference? That's huge. Too many people focus on the words they say and don't take enough responsibility for how those words are received.

You are blessed when you have smaller crowds where you can instantly see people's reactions to your messages: the expressions on their faces, their smiles, their tears, etc. You are able to witness their attentiveness, or you can see if they start to glaze over, and you immediately have an opportunity to intensify your engagement. This is a great arena to hone your skills. Even if you have advanced to speaking to large audiences—or perhaps especially if you have—taking time to speak to more intimate groups helps you improve your skills, strengthen your messaging and timing, and see what is and isn't working by witnessing first-hand in real time how your audience is receiving you.

I have spent the majority of my career speaking in front of television and movie cameras, and others have often commented that my presence feels so personal. Part of that has to do with the fact that, especially as a woman, I cannot stand being talked at—I want someone to talk *to* me. I bring that purpose with me every time I communicate. I also have thirty years of experience as an actress, including working with esteemed acting coaches, and twelve years working with a prestigious improv troupe, not to mention years spent in my childhood with a speech coach overcoming a speech impediment brought on by years of wearing braces. Throughout all of this, there is one thread that ties it all together, and that is my passion to communicate, not just speak.

Communicating is a little different in that it emphasizes delivering and receiving together, taking into account how the audience feels about what is being said, knowing that how messages are received are just as important as how they are conveyed. As Maya Angelou is widely credited for saying, *"People may forget what you say, but they'll always remember how you made them feel."*

Most people render content, and they try to pack in data and information that is often overwhelming, complex, or difficult to process, absorb, and remember. My goal has always been different: to affect audiences on a visceral level, for them to think and reflect throughout the journey of my talk and come to profound conclusions on their own.

Substantial content is there, but it's the delivery, the technique, and understanding the outcome that truly drives the work I do and teach. One of the greatest compliments I often receive from participants in my audiences is when they reach out to me and feel the need to tell me their personal stories. They feel an intimate connection, and they open up to me with beautiful messages of overcoming heart-wrenching obstacles and how something I said reached inside, touched them, and resonated with them, causing them to take positive action in their lives as they reclaim their purpose, health, self-respect and importance in the world. When that happens, I feel I have done my job.

My belief is that "speaking" is an art of telling stories that drives home great content. However, it's also important to remember that for the most part, people have short attention spans.

With the expanse of YouTube, cell phones, and the like, this is a cultural shift that speakers must clearly understand and embrace. Just watch CNN, and notice that while you're hearing a news report, there are several breaking news updates streaming at the bottom of your screen simultaneously. We are now so accustomed to taking in gargantuan amounts of information at once, that spending considerable time trying to take in one detailed message seems challenging. While most people in an audience mean to be fully attentive, supportive, and respectful of speakers in front of them, the reality is that we as a society are forever distracted. Not just from media feeds but also from our countless electronic devices demanding our attention, then add to that challenging schedules and responsibilities, and personal and professional worries. Staying focused for prolong periods just doesn't come easily to most of us anymore, if it ever did.

As a speaker—someone dedicated to communicating with your audience—your job is not to fight this battle of attention spans or to scold your audience for succumbing to their nature but to learn strategies to work with this cultural shift. When appropriate (or sometimes maybe when it's not appropriate), pepper a little humor throughout your delivery. It doesn't matter what it is—a silly joke here or there is fine. A humorous, mildly self-deprecating tale that helps humanize you can also be effective. This does two things: 1) it gives your audience a break from a potentially daunting amount of content and 2) it reengages them, refreshing their attention by breaking up the style of the messages they have been receiving thus far.

Another strategy is to simplify your content. Remember, it's not likely that you're presenting at a research seminar, and even if you are, believe me when I say that even researchers who present on content could benefit from this advice. Break apart your content into small segments and tell meaningful stories to drive home the data you want remembered. This is where qualitative and quantitative evidence merges. Use your facts to tell stories that have an emotional hook, are memorable, and repeatable.

⋛ *Brilliant Quick Tip* ⋚

Simplify your content: break it into small segments and tell meaningful stories and personal truths to drive home what you want remembered.

I personally tend to look at the world from a 30,000 foot view—I examine content and patterns on a broad scale, and that allows me to connect dots that others may not see who are looking at things up close. I also love to see the world from the eyes of a six year old. When I look at content from a child-like perspective, there's a playfulness, wonder, and excitement that I use to examine it and then talk from the heart. I went to

college and earned two degrees, but I still prefer elementary school. I think the lessons we learned there are stronger: how to share, to play nicely, to have good sportsmanship, to explore things and to have fun. I often deliver messages from a bag of stories I've collected to help drive home profound lessons that have impacted me in my life. From near death experiences and overcoming odds, to wild moments of seemingly impossible synchronicity—these stories touch people, and they share them and think about them later.

Tie in your personal truth, because that is something that will always be original to you, and no one else can take credit for it: your lived experiences and lessons learned through the winding paths you've experienced on your journey. Use your life as a metaphor.

These stories are something no one can ever take from you. I was asked to be the keynote speaker at a women's retreat a couple of years ago, and I spoke to a lively group of accomplished professional women. Intuitively, I knew they didn't want me preaching to them, spewing off lists of what they could do, or worse, *should* do to get more from their lives or whatever so many tired "motivational speeches" tend to do. I thought about events in my life that have served as the foundation of some of my most profound teachable moments, and I shared stories. One of these stories included a lesson that I had learned about manifesting what I want, no matter how impossible it seemed. When I was done, the crew that I had hired to accompany me on this trip looked at me and asked, *"What was that all about? You just talked about yourself."* I started to explain myself, and before I really did explain myself, I stopped. I knew what I had done reached my intended audience—I saw it in their faces.

Then, during the same retreat following my speech, the group had gathered for a raffle. Among the items available was a piece of jewelry, and one of the women there was so excited about the possibility of winning it—her daughter was getting married, and this would be perfect with her outfit. Even I was thinking, wow, that's a long shot! With all of these women here, what are the chances this specific woman will win this specific piece of jewelry? And then as the raffle numbers were announced—yep. She won! As she won this, she turned to me and said, *"Oh my God! I Forbes'd it!"*

Suddenly a new verb was born. To "Forbes it" is to manifest something, especially if all the odds are against you. This came from my speech that my crew thought was meaningless, selfish, and all about me. Use your stories to impact your audience, unapologetically. Know and grow to understand the value of your messaging and your unique voice. If your intended audience is impacted and you ultimately get what you want, you've done your job. You don't owe people who don't understand you . . . your message wasn't for them. Dare to trailblaze and trust your instincts.

You are the only you on this planet, and your voice and what you have to offer is needed. Own that and offer that to the world as your ultimate platform.

That is not to say that you shouldn't listen to or even emulate others in some ways. There is always room to improve, tweak, amplify, hone in on subtleties, etc. One great tool that we have available to us is the Internet. You can conjure up some of the greatest speakers of our day and even our past to examine and study their mastery. How do they look, what do they wear, how do they stand, how do they move, what are their facial expressions, what's their body language? Then, look at other examples of them speaking—from the past to the present. How has their look changed? What works best for them? Really examine this, then see if you can apply some of this to yourself.

⟩ *Brilliant Quick Tip* ⟨

Use the Internet to study the mastery
of some of the great speakers of our
day and our past.

Beyond physical appearance and mannerisms, how do they sound? How do they harness the power of their voice—is it soft or loud? How do they use inflection? What about pauses and moments of silence? Sometimes the absence of talking can say even more than filling in all the spaces. What about word choices—what level of vocabulary do they use, do they utilize mostly empowering words or fear-inducing words to motivate? How well did their strategies work? Would you benefit from trying some of these strategies?

There are many other specific exercises and techniques that I use to coach speakers, but overall, I will end with emphasizing where we began: How does what you say land in the heart of those listening to you? If you're pleased with your answer to that question, congratulations! You're already 100 steps ahead of the game. If not, what do you want?

About Forbes Riley

Forbes Riley is an award-winning television host, National Fitness Hall of Fame inductee, author, sought-after spokesperson and keynote speaker, and coach to celebrities and entrepreneurs. She has helped millions through her unshakeable beliefs on the impact of a healthy lifestyle.

Highlighted by *Forbes* magazine as being a megabrand CEO for her SpinGym®, Forbes has gained international celebrity status from her globally broadcasted infomercials for Jack Lalanne Juicer, Living Well Healthmaster Blender, and more than 142 other half-hour infomercials, which have grossed hundreds of millions of dollars. She's recognized worldwide on *HSN* and *QVC*. A pioneer in the TV host field, Forbes debuted by hosting the ESPN series, *The X-Games*, hosting for three years alongside Stuart Scott. Following, she was the original host of *Fit TV* with Jake "Body by Jake" Steinfeld.

In 2010 Forbes created SpinGym, a handheld spinning device that received a US patent for her innovative exercises. SpinGym launched on NBCs, *The Doctors*. Forbes has sold over 1.5 million of them.

Today she's launched a series called *Forbes Living*, seen on *WE-TV*. She shares her time with her twelve year old boy and girl twins, between Los Angeles and St Petersburg, Florida.

Learn more about Forbes Riley at:
ForbesRiley.com

4

⸙Brilliant Advice⸙
from Jim Ross Meskimen

The Enduring Value of a Live Speaker

Back in the days of what author Kurt Vonnegut once dubbed "bow-wow oratory," early in our nation's history, speakers would hold forth for hours without any artificial amplification at all outside of perhaps a large megaphone for groups of citizens who would brave the elements, waiting patiently on picnic blankets or atop split rail fences to hear what the "great man" (and back then, it was almost always exclusively a great man) had on his mind.

When Daniel Webster gave his Plymouth Oration, for example, way back in 1820, commemorating the Bicentennial of the pilgrim's landing at Plymouth Rock in Massachusetts, he spoke outdoors to thousands for what must have been hours, recounting the highlights of the 200 years just passed, in formal scholarly prose that even included long passages in Latin.

Obviously, the attention span of the audience of 1820 was not what we encounter today; the pace of the period was calibrated to the rising and the setting sun, not the glow of iPhones.

But where Webster's feat was an Olympic event compared to what is required of today's speakers, the same principles apply to one mounting the podium in the Twenty-first Century as to those hardy speakers of yore who, mounting a tree stump, tried to win over a crowd.

And whereas listening to a live speaker in 1820 was one of the very few ways that ordinary people could share in the big ideas of the day, today the super-abundance of communication channels, repositories, and relayers of big ideas, many times far outstrips the quality of the ideas themselves. As we depend more and more on canned and even digitally generated information, people gather far less frequently to hear someone actually speak in person than perhaps ever in the history of our species.

Why then, do they show up at all? And what gives a live speaker such enduring value?

No One Sees Through Your Eyes

One obvious fundamental is that we like to know what other people are thinking. We have a voracious appetite for the points of view of others.

We want to learn new things, to have our understandings broadened, clarified, or challenged.

We want to hear the thoughts of people we agree with, and even those with whom we disagree.

Often we care to hear someone distill data for us, so that we can make a judgment without having to wade thru a swamp of information ourselves. And of course, we all love a story.

"I'll never forget the time when . . ." is instantly arresting to the listener, and indeed can create a listener when before there was none. It's the thinly veiled equivalent to childhood's *"Once upon a time . . ."*

Any story is better than no story. Even hearing a poor story becomes a good story in itself, as the listener/victim can make it a good story by recounting the painful event at a later date, (or five minutes after on Twitter).

A really good story is, of course, the fundamental of almost all art, and even grand movements in history, such as major religions. A story personalizes the "Big Ideas" of life, brings them down to street level, and dresses them up in clothes that we recognize from our own closets.

A good story has specifics, as opposed to generalities. Are your stories rich in detail? Make sure you paint a clear and descriptive picture; let the audience "see it" and they will become more involved.

⋛ *Brilliant Quick Tip* ⋚

Paint a clear and descriptive picture with your stories; let the audience "see it" and they will become more involved.

Good stories are said to be rare—that all the good ones have already been told and audiences have long since grown irrevocably bored with their echoes. Oh, yeah? Tell that to the producers of the latest Batman reboot.

No, I believe stories are by their very nature an evergreen affair, since they provide something that every person who ever took a breath desires: to receive an invitation to step outside the dreary, everyday world.

Another fundamental fact worth having a look at in this context is that most of us have a tendency to consider that everybody is just like us. We assume that the random person on the street holds dear the same values we do, or has the same aspirations, or views the world in the same way we do. This, I'm afraid, is as silly as thinking that everyone prefers the same foods, pets, or films.

The fact is, everyone occupies a unique place in the universe, and we all have a unique view of life that is entirely our own. We may be "like" the multitude, but we are truly only exactly like ourselves.

The experiences of your life are similar to those of others, but they are singular and special. And those experiences you have had, viewpoints you have held, observations you have made, and conclusions you have reached, occurred only after innumerable small events and decisions had transpired, that you alone had a hand in.

You've been on a path that factually no one else has traveled, though you have been able to view others traveling similar paths nearby that paralleled and often intertwined with your own.

What have people most often ask you about your field? Address those questions early in your talk and lead them into a broader understanding.

≳ *Brilliant Quick Tip* ≲

Address the most burning questions early in your talk, and then lead the audience on to a broader understanding.

Learn While Being Taught

What you sow as a speaker you may also reap; when you share your unique experiences and viewpoints in a talk you will gain understanding from the audience, just as they themselves gain understanding and a new viewpoint. They will tell you, with their attention, with their applause, with their shifting in their chairs and indeed their yawns, what they have accepted from your speech and what has frankly left them unmoved, bored, or confused.

It takes some courage to put yourself out there, armed with only your experiences and a PowerPoint, but in taking that risk, you will learn and teach at the same moment.

≥ *Brilliant Quick Tip* ≤

In taking the risk to put yourself out there as a speaker, the gift is that you will learn and teach at the same moment.

Another thing worth mentioning is that the fuse is burning on the time you have left to reach out and touch people with your stories and experiences. In the high speed world of the Twenty-first Century culture, there are only so many opportunities to get up in front of people and let them know what you are most concerned about, or find charming, or are afraid of.

An idea is a valuable thing, but only if it is communicated. Your ideas have value, and can fulfill the possibility of changing the lives of others in a positive way.

So, here I hope I have emphasized two reasons to put a fire under yourself to create your talk and get busy, to get heard by people, to reach out and build your audience: 1) that your experiences are almost always going to be new to people, no matter how ordinary they may be to you, and 2) that you need to start right away to get in front of people and share your ideas now, because time is always your enemy, and great things left unsaid have no chance of influencing anybody; like the un-purchased Lotto ticket or the kiss one lacked courage to attempt, there can be nothing gained.

Back in 1820, after Daniel Webster had taken his standing ovations (and probably horseback-mounted ovations) and repaired to the nearest public house to sooth his stentorian throat with ale, his opinion of the events and participants of the preceding 200 years became as solid as a legal precedent, and indeed formed a lens through which the American past was viewed by generations to come.

Which of your own views would you desire to survive long after you are gone?

And, by the way, do you own a megaphone?

About Jim Ross Meskimen

As a professional actor for nearly thirty years, Jim Meskimen has appeared in the films *Apollo 13*, *The Grinch*, *Frost/Nixon*, *There Will Be Blood*, and many others. Jim's television credits include *Parks & Recreation*, *Friends*, and *Whose Line is it, Anyway*? He currently stars in *The Impression Guys* on the SoulPancake channel on YouTube. His impressionist video, *Shakespeare in Celebrity Voices* went viral in 2011. Scott Simon, on NPR's *Weekend Edition* dubbed him, "*The Greatest Impressionist of our times.*"

Meskimen lives in Los Angeles. His mother is actress Marion Ross, "Mrs. C" of *Happy Days* fame.

Learn more about JimRossMeskimen at:
JimMeskimen.com

5

≥Brilliant Advice≤
from Carla Ferrer

*Inject Your Personality and Brand to Create
an Unforgettable Audience Experience*

In today's world of public speaking, standing out from the crowd is one of your first priorities in establishing a career at the podium. Your success depends on it.

In order to market yourself and your own individuality, you must have something that sets you apart from all others.

What is your specialty? What is your niche? Whether your material is very similar to most seen and heard today or uniquely distinct, your personalized delivery is undoubtedly your strength.

While people won't remember everything that you say in a program, they will remember who you were being while you presented. Thus, if your wish is to be one of those speakers people talk about long after the program is over, here are a few innovative suggestions for how you can inject your personality and brand to create an unforgettable experience for your audience.

Tip #1: *Tell your Signature Story*

Nothing is better than a good story. Weaving your signature stories into the core of your message turns an ordinary talk into a real crowd pleaser. For example, my story is one of underdog to overcomer, wherein I share it with a message of hope for anyone who wants to be unstoppable—rising above any and all circumstances, enjoying ultimate success whether that means losing weight to be healthy and live life to its fullest, or to reach a milestone financial goal. Simply put, I've entwined my personal story with a direct message to the audience about determination and intention . . . and the power held within our attitudes.

Do you have a turning point in your life that shaped you into the person you are? Do you have a "rags to riches story"? Make a list of your trademark stories that you could share in presentations.

Once you've determined the key point(s) to your story, I suggest you create a hook from the start. As Lyndon Johnson once said about audiences, *"If they're with you at the takeoff, they'll be with you in the landing."* Therefore, find a way to capture your audience's attention in the first thirty seconds with a provocative statement, a thought-provoking question, or a relevant anecdote that sets up the topic or material you are planning to discuss. It also can be helpful to utilize a "teaser," such as asking a question you don't answer right away or "teasing" a topic that will be detailed later in your presentation. Withholding certain facts or information will build suspense with your audience and will keep them with you from start to finish.

Tip #2: *Highlight the Benefit*

"What's in it for me?" This is what every audience is thinking at the start of your training or presentation. Audiences always will be looking for a tangible benefit you can provide to them with the message you are delivering, so don't be shy about stating concrete and specific details about how your program or

plan could have a positive effect on productivity or the bottom line.

How will it save them time, save them money, or make their job or life easier? Clearly and equivocally spell out the benefit you are providing for those giving you their time and attention.

Tip #3: *Don't be Afraid to Show Your Flaws*

One of the things we sometimes forget as "experts" is that it's okay to show your vulnerability. In fact, sharing your weaknesses can actually build credibility and trust. For instance, when I step up to the front of the room, no one would ever guess that at one time I was a morbidly obese woman weighing in at 330 pounds. Leading with this as an "opener" immediately gets the audience's attention . . . and from there I let my story unfold.

Do you have a story about a challenge you faced or a hard learned mistake? People really admire when you are not afraid to show your "warts" like that. You know, no one is perfect. Everyone starts from somewhere. And when we see that someone has overcome great obstacles like that it gives us hope.

> ≥ *Brilliant Quick Tip* ≤
>
> *Be willing to show your vulnerabilities.*
> *It gives people hope to know others*
> *have overcome obstacles.*

Tip #4: *Create a Signature Presentation Style and Look that's All Your Own*

For example, in my case, my message is one of health and wellness with dramatic physical transformation, thus part of my branding was always to appear dressed wearing very form fitting yoga wear (LuLu Lemmon). Or even if you just want to position yourself as a world-class speaker, having a polished looking suit or even wearing a tie in your brand colors can set you apart.

Tip #5: *Pull Your Hobbies and Interests into Your Program*

Watch Monday night football and you know that people get pretty passionate about their sports. That's why weaving your interests, hobbies, and pets into your speaking programs turns regular audience members into raving fans.

Think about what fun or unique things you would share about yourself during your programs. Do you love dancing? Are you a dog lover? Do you love sports? By tying these personal facts into your program you add instant interest.

> ≳ *Brilliant Quick Tip* ≲
>
> *To add interest to your program, tie in some personal interests or hobbies the audience can relate to.*

Tip #6: *Add Your Unique Brand of Humor*

Humor has the power to transform an ordinary program into a fun experience for the whole audience. For some speakers, their humor bits become their trademark. Case in point, when I begin to speak on the subject of "dieting" (the mere word repels me) I make a point to humorously state that I don't want to diet, I've done every diet, and I'm clearly not a rabbit, thus surviving on carrots is not an option!

Tip #7: *Share Your Own Quotes*

Often speakers get caught up in sharing the famous words of other speakers. Why not leave the audience with your words as the final thought? Before you know it people will be quoting *you* in articles and speeches. You can create your own quotes to share during presentations, as instant quotes for the media, and to add to your handouts.

Here's one from my book that shares my belief that *"When you declare yourself unstoppable, you can bridge the gap between impossible and attainable. Therefore, change your attitude and your life will change!"*

Tip #8: *Your Delivery is Just as Important as Your Content*

News flash! Perfecting your script is not enough. It's imperative to understand that equally important to the content of your presentation (and branding) is your delivery of it. Here are some key dos and don'ts for you to apply every time you're at the front of the room:

a) No Apologies: never start a presentation with an apology. How many times have you heard a presenter begin by saying *"I am sorry I have a cold,"* or *"I am nervous?"* If you have a cold, the sniffles do a fine job of making that apparent. Or, if there are no outward signs, who really needs to know you don't feel well? Many people use such statements as a way of requesting leniency from the audience. Apologies like this announce to the audience, *"the presentation you are about to receive is less than you deserve, but please don't blame me."*

b) *Attention:* get and keep their attention. Different people have different learning styles. Some learn by simply listening, some need to see it, and some learn best by experiencing it. If appropriate, try to fit all aspects into the presentation. Visual aides are a great way to keep your audience's attention.

c) *Move:* make the most of your movement. I appreciate the value of high energy and enthusiasm. Many of my presentations incorporate both strategies. At times however, too much high-energy and movement can be distracting, actually taking away from your message. Appropriate use of movement is the key. Simple hand gestures may be all you need to make a point. On the other hand, sometimes it may take running around the room. Your movement is most effective when it helps the audience connect to your subject.

d) *Voice:* use your voice to make your point. It seems obvious: use your voice when you are speaking. Well, here are some specific tips on *how* to use it:

᠈ Speak up! Nothing takes away from a great presentation more than having audience members acting like a commercial for Miracle Ear, *"What'd he say?"*

᠈ Have someone stand in the back of the room and signal if you need to be louder.

᠈ No fillers—similar to foods, the best presentations have no fillers. That is, no *"um's,"* or *"uh's"* to fill the space between when you think of something and when you actually say it.

᠈ Silence between statements allows your audience to process what you said.

᠈ Switch it up—to emphasize a point, speak louder or even speak softer; the change in volume will get the audience's attention.

d) *Respect:* show respect to the audience and they will show it to you. Remember, the audience wants you to do well, and the smallest amount of respect will win over even the toughest of critics. Similar to one-on-one conversations, showing respect to people can make all the difference in the communication. Here are some ways to demonstrate respect for your audience:

᠈ Eye contact—maintain eye contact with the audience. Slowly move from person to person and occasionally hold the contact for a few seconds.

᠈ Honesty—when you don't know the answer, admit it, offer to find out, and get back to the person.

≳ Save face—if you must disagree with an audience member, do so in a manner that allows the person to save face.

≳ Self-correction—if an audience member is not paying attention, encourage self-correction, by walking closer to them as you speak. The "distracter" will notice your proximity and stop the distraction.

f) *Pause for Effect*: we think at a much faster rate than our optimal speaking rate, so it is important to consciously slow down your pace when speaking to an audience. This is something that is not always easy to do when the adrenaline starts to flow. It takes concentration and focus, but make sure you slow down your speaking pace so your words have a greater impact for your audience. Remember, in most cases, they are hearing this information for the first time, so they need to hear and consider what you are saying. As a trainer or presenter, don't be afraid of silence. Pause at specific points to let the information you are providing sink in with your audience.

≳ *Brilliant Quick Tip* ≲

Don't be afraid of silence in your presentation. Pause occasionally to let the information sink in for your audience.

As anyone with the task of delivering a message to others knows, you need to penetrate your audience to make an impact on them. While facilitating a meeting, delivering feedback, or leading a training session, without engagement—meaning your audience is in a willing state of attentiveness—effective communication is not possible. It doesn't matter who you are or what topic you are discussing, if the arrow that is your message does not hit its intended target, you will have fallen short of the mark as a communicator. So don't rely on your data or visual aids alone to engage an audience. And while the words and information are an important piece of the engagement puzzle, by incorporating what I have shared into your delivery, you will be well on your way to capturing your audience's attention and changing the way they think or behave.

In summary, as you strive to develop your recognition as a professional speaker, perfecting your style and delivery, I suggest you brand yourself in the process, as it will be that much easier for people to remember you and recommend you as well. In as much, choose your brand carefully and then see if you can get the domain name for it as well as your own personal name. For example, I have my name, CarlaFerrer.com, as well as my book: FatToFanTabulous.com, and also my weight loss program: CoachCarlaWeightLoss.com

Know that memorable speakers have one thing in common; they know how to create a connection with their listeners. Therefore, the most important thing for you to remember is that if you want your audience to remember you, your presentation is obviously the most valuable gift you can give them. So, don't just have *information* that is amazing . . . *you* be amazing; be a servant speaker who connects with the audience in an authentic, compelling, and compassionate manner. Be fantabulous!

About Carla Ferrer

Carla Ferrer is an author, successful entrepreneur, keynote speaker, and National Presidential Director, corporate trainer, and Fitness Ambassador with IDLife.

A seasoned entrepreneur and life coach in the field of transformation and consciousness for healthy and affluent lifestyle living, Carla has over twenty years experience empowering profound personal and professional breakthroughs for men and women throughout the United States and the United Kingdom.

Carla marries her depth of wisdom and insight, with passion, humor, and sensitivity, to empower individuals in living a life by design that is rich and strong in every way.

Learn more about Carla Ferrer at:
CarlaFerrer.com

6

≳Brilliant Advice≲
from Tracy Repchuk

The Money Maker That's Either for You or Against You

As a speaker in over thirty-five countries, there is much I have seen on and off the stage. The most devastating thing never happens on the stage, though, it happens right from where your money comes.

I meet the most amazing speakers, coaches, authors, and entrepreneurs all around the world: successful, well-dressed, great speakers, professional—and then it happens.

I want to recommend them, people want to hire them and use their services. It's the exact reason they were there: to make an impact and an impression; to touch and reach people with their message; and to make money, either by paid speaking gigs, or selling their services.

Either way—nothing replaces a first impression right? It's why you dress for the part and look professional. Then why do so many speakers, authors, coaches, and businesses have a website that is failing them professionally?

If your websites aren't working for you, they're working against you! Read that line again—it is that important.

> *If your websites aren't working for you,
> they're working against you!*

You have three seconds to make an impression and if you don't look as good online as you do off, you're losing money, customers, and wasting your most valuable marketing.

To be successful online, you need to be able to navigate the Internet through wrong data, confusing steps, and the misleading hype about what you should be doing for your business to attract more leads, get more clients, and make more sales.

Social media has transformed the landscape. Search engine optimization (SEO) is even more vital, and brand management is at a premium, and together they combine to give you the cohesive strategy you need to make an *Instant Online Impact.*

You see, historically, companies *were* the brand, and people stood behind that. That game has changed because the Internet and audiences want to be able to identify the person behind it all. They want to know who they would hire or work with, because the Internet became so overwhelming there needed to be a way to connect and engage.

So the person moved from behind the company and started to stand in front. Especially as a speaker—*you* are the brand.

This created a problem though—the person did not always become the brand, but often sent mixed messages representing the company and themselves. Yet, when a person became fully branded, this is when it changed and success was imminent.

After spending thirty years in technology, marketing, and branding, and twenty years on the Internet, I have a unique ability to bring all the elements together to create a cohesive end-to-end structure where you:

> ≥ Match professionally

> ≥ Rise above the competition

> ≥ Reach millions with your message

Your website needs to make you look credible and like the authority you are by profiling you in such a way that you are unique, understood, and focused on your target market. You should look as good online as you do off.

≳ *Brilliant Quick Tip* ≲

Your website is often the first impression others have of you online. Ensure that it profiles you clearly—as the expert you are—to your desired target.

Branding is beyond a logo: it's the consistency in how you use it. It's a way to equalize your identity online, and allows you to compete against the biggest brands in the world and capture your market space. A brand is what your customer perceives you to be and do. This is why it's so important that you put out the brand you want them to perceive and believe is *you*. Project the image you want so your customer can feel, relate to, and believe you—in everything you do.

When you don't take time to establish your brand and integrate it into your online assets, your customer will determine what it is, and it can be perceived differently by every one of them, thus confusing your target audience completely.

The easiest way to win is to match the expectations of your target market, and be clear and consistent from end to end.

Branding is the consistent message you convey to your customers verbally, visually, and emotionally. You have just seconds to make an impact, and your brand is where it needs to begin. Your brand should resonate with your target market at every level, and be unique to you.

> ⋛ *Brilliant Quick Tip* ⋚
>
> *Determine what you want to be known for. Then work everything around that.*

Your brand has to take the lead. *You* determine—*what do you want to be known for?* Then work everything around *that*. There are eight parts to being *Brand You*:

1. Your USP—Unique Selling Proposition

Then taking the expectations of your target market you determine 2-8.

2. Your colors

3. Your logo

4. Your Website—first impression (the look and feel of your website)

5. You—first impression (your personal look to match your brand)

6. How you treat your customers (build loyalty, bond)

7. How you behave in public (your actions speak louder than words)

8. How and what you communicate (blog, emails, social media, phone, marketing, business card)

Your USP is the force that drives your business and success. It can also be used as a "branding" tool that deploys strategy through your marketing. This allows you to build a lasting reputation while you're making sales. The ultimate goal of your USP and marketing is to have people instantly understand what you do and how you can help them.

So as a speaker, there are two types of website layouts you can use depending on the type of speaker you are.

If you're a keynote speaker, and professional speaking is your *major sole source* of revenue, devote your entire website to you as a speaker. This is clearly *Brand You Speaker*. Here, it's critical to show your *Unique Selling Proposition (USP),* because you are being compared to all the other speakers. Therefore, *why they should choose you* should be clear.

When you use speaking as a lead generation tool, an *additional* financial resource, and it's a small part of what you do, your website is even more complex, as it is probably selling services, products, *and* you as a speaker. In this case, it's critical your message and USP is very clear *and* also integrated into all you do. Otherwise you may overwhelm a visitor, confuse them, and lose more than a speaking gig; you could lose the lifetime value of a customer.

When you have the complex model just mentioned, you need a master site, and a domain to point to your speaker page within your master site. This way, when you are specifically promoting yourself as a speaker, you can send you're your contact directly to your speaker page so they don't get distracted and have to search for it. My master site is TracyRepchuk.com, and an example of a domain pointing to a speaker page is TracyRepchukLive.com

⋛ *Brilliant Quick Tip* ⋚

If speaking is your lead generation tool, have a domain pointing to your speaker page from within your master website.

The biggest mistake I find is website, logo, and brand colors that don't match the target market expectation. I have gone to websites that service women only to find colors that are dark and black. I have gone to sites that target men and found mauve and orange. And it goes on and on.

When you are selecting colors, do not pick just what you like. This isn't about you. You are *Brand You*, but you need to match the expectations of your target market or you will have an immediate disconnect, and although your visitor won't be able to say why, they will leave.

The key is to carry your colors (the right colors), your USP, and your logo across your websites and social media, so you cater to the expectations of your target market. In addition, keep your navigation clean, and your message clear. Make it easy to buy what you sell and understand what you do.

Almost ninety percent of the websites out there are not created with marketing in mind, and site owners have been ill advised on structure, navigation, colors, and layout.

So don't fall in love with something out there and want your website and branding to look that way. First, know what will work best for you with respect to selling you, your products, your services, and attracting speaking gigs. Once you know how to do it, you'll be able to choose the right pieces that will best serve you, and you will look as great online as you do offline.

And this may be a learning process for you. Know that it's okay to change, evolve, grow, and transition through many phases of *Brand You*, as long as you keep your target market expectations in mind.

Last but not least, let's touch on what should be on your speaker page (webpage). The primary elements are:

⋛ Your specific speaker bio (different than about section)

⋛ Your speaker reel

⋛ Your signature talk (with details on how it would be listed on a program)

⋛ Upcoming events

⋛ Past speaking engagements

⋛ Photos of you (that can be accessed for promotion)

⋛ Testimonials and recommendations (if you have them)

Optional features:

- Calendar for directly booking you

- Your rate sheet

- Your speaker one sheet (download link)

- A couple of promo videos

Now, take a look at your website and ask yourself, "*Do I look as professional online as I do offline*?" If not, give me a call and get fully branded from end-to-end in under sixty days.

About Tracy Repchuk

Tracy Repchuk is an international best-selling author, an online marketing and social media strategist, and speaker. An award-winning entrepreneur since the age of nineteen, with over thirty years of business, Internet, SEO, and marketing background, Tracy has helped thousands of clients get their presence and message online fast and effectively. In addition, she has appeared as a technology specialist in national TV segments with *ABC7, San Diego Living, Good Morning New Mexico, CNBC, 4 Your Money, Report on Business, HGTV, FOX, ABC, NBC, KMIR, Daytime, Fox 5 Las Vegas, New Mexico Style, Vegas Inc, The CW, USA Today, Forbes, MSN Money, King5, CW,* and over fifty publications, newspapers, and magazines, plus two motivational movies and hundreds of speaking appearances in over thirty-five countries.

Learn more about Tracy Repchuk at:
TracyRepchuk.com

65

7

⹂Brilliant Advice⹂
from Caterina Rando

Produce Your Own Live Events— Gain Clients with Ease

You can produce your own live seminars and events to gain insta-clients with ease. I want to help you get started!

The challenge with being a professional speaker is that when you get booked, in most cases your speaking gig only lasts one day. Even when you do a great job, many groups do not want to have you back again for another year—if you are lucky—and often, they do not want to have you back for two years because they want different speakers at their next events.

Of course as a speaker, you want to be speaking, not spending countless hours dialing for dollars, trying to get booked. So, instead of relying on others to book you, book yourself, and become as busy speaking as you want to be. The way to do that is by producing your own seminars and events.

For the last few years I have been producing over ninety days of my own events. I have seen firsthand that holding your own live and in-person trainings, events, and group programs can catapult your business faster than anything.

While it can be wonderful for a time to be a speaker who jets from city to city, conference to conference, the glamour wears off after a while, especially when it interferes with being with your family. Part of the value of producing your own events is that *you* choose where you do your own programs. This allows you the option to eliminate a lot of your airplane and travel time by hosting your events and trainings in the area where you live.

Your own seminars and events can include everything from a two-hour introduction workshop, to a one-day or two-day seminar, to a multi-speaker conference, to an on-going training program with several days of meetings. Whichever way you want to deliver your value, get started now.

Before we go any further, I want to address a concern you may be having. I see too many speakers who want to do their own seminars, group programs, and events, yet they are waiting . . . telling themselves they are not "there" yet. "There" might be the place where they feel they are a better or more polished speaker, or "there" might be the place where the list is bigger or they are better known. "There" might be the future with many more hours of time on the platform. What I want to say very clearly is that doing your own seminars, events, and group programs will get you "there" faster and more quickly than anything else. You will become a more masterful speaker by doing your own events and booking yourself more than anyone else will book you. It is time for you to get in action with your own events and seminars.

I have for you here proven strategies to get you started on your path to massively monetizing in your business with intro events.

All You Need to Get Started

Far too many speakers spend months planning even the simplest event. When you do this, you push off the revenue from those events. All you need is a date, a price, and a topic to start to talk about your event and to sell it. Yes, you need a name and a brand and a place to hold your event, but you do not need that to get started. Once you have a price and a date, and you sign up your first person, you will have more focus and energy to get in action around everything else you need. Sheila, a speaker client of mine, said she would do her first seminar in six months. I told her to do it in six weeks, she did, and in six months she had produced six of her own seminars, served many with her wisdom, and was more certain about her business and her ability to earn well with her own seminars and events!

⋛ *Brilliant Quick Tip* ⋚

To get started hosting your own events, all you need is a date, a price, and a topic. Then you can begin to sell it!

Don't Go too Big too Soon

Often speakers tell me they want to host a week-long seminar in a far away city. That sounds like a wonderful adventure.

Recognize it is a lot harder to fill a week-long program when you have not yet sold a one-day or a two-day program. I encourage everyone to start with a two-hour seminar, then go to a half-day, then a full-day, then a two-day. Starting with three days or more will make your job of selling out very challenging.

Make Sure Your Venue Matches

Find a venue that is brand consistent for you and your event. Pick a place where your ideal clients will feel comfortable visiting. Use your network to find a venue that will be affordable, yet still reflects well on you and your business. Often hotels will give you meeting rooms for a low fee or no fee when you guarantee a certain number of meeting rooms or purchase catering.

Cultivate Champions

Make a list of your clients, friends, and referral partners who think you and your work are awesome and who want to spread the word about what you are up to. Champions have to be people who have the same values as you, people you like a lot, and who are your ideal clients. Champions with influence or a big network, who are loud and proud about the value you bring, are especially recommended. Call and email your champions and let them know what you are up to and ask them to support your event.

Make it easy for your champions to support your event. Write social media posts for them, Set them up as affiliates, and give them an affiliate link to register their friends. This ensures the registrants are tracked back to the champion who invited them (the referral source), so you can pay them a commission. You should pay your champions a commission so they will keep referring people to your events.

﹥ Brilliant Quick Tip ﹤

Make a list of people who support you and love what you do. These are your champions. Pay them a commission for each person they bring to your event.

Get Great Support

Have your staff—or even trusted volunteers—come early and stay late, to help you check in the guests and make them feel welcome.

You will want to have your attention on your program and on selling, not on setting up, adjusting the room temperature, and making sure everyone has a seat. You are the speaker, and you will need to focus. There will be people who will want to ask you questions after your speech. You will need a couple of people to take orders and to help answer some of the more basic questions. You will also need help setting up and breaking down.

Set the Stage

Run your business and your events for where your business is going, not for where you are currently. Have the same care and amenities you would for a big event. What that means is signage, flowers, music, nametags, and branded binders if your budget allows.

Remember, often people are meeting you for the first time. Make a great first impression on all counts. Sharon, a speaker-client of mine, always greets everyone personally as they walk in the room, making them feel welcome; and she says it makes audience members more open to what she has to say when she begins her program.

Use Multiple Tools to Fill Your Events

The biggest challenge with doing your own events is filling the room. Not to worry, use a variety of strategies to ensure you have a full room every time. Here are some of my favorites:

> Hold a free tele-class or webinar and share some of the content from the event. Then invite people to attend to get more. People are curious and want to see how much value you have to bring, and when you share great tips on your tele-class or webinar, many will be confident they will receive more at your live event.

> Create a special event landing page on your website that includes information about the program and links to register. Use this as a way to capture names and build your mailing list for future events.

> Plan a special live event . . . for your live event. It is harder to fill the room for a one or two-day event than for a short session. You can do so with ease by holding a two-hour workshop as an introductory event. This gives people a chance to meet you personally and learn what they will gain by joining you for your event. The intro event is highly effective. It allows your champions to put many people in front of you because they are only

asking people who do not know you to give up a couple of hours. When you do a great job with your intro event and you offer a discount for people to sign up for your upcoming event, you will get many signups in the room, thereby filling your bigger events.

⋛ Make a list of all past clients you think would be great to attend. Reach out to them—your personal invitation can generate more sales than a series of free tele-calls or email blasts.

⋛ Create an email sequence to get the word out and invite people to register. Once they register, guess what? You still have to keep enrolling them so they show up. You will want a separate email sequence for the people who have already registered as well.

⋛ Pick up the phone. With all of the technology today, the simplicity of picking up the phone often gets over-looked. A personal phone call inviting someone to the event personalizes the invitations, which carries a lot more weight than ten times the social media invites and emails, and get much better results.

⋛ *Brilliant Quick Tip* ⋚

Use all available tools to fill your events, including a free tele-class or a short, live workshop. Use the phone to personally reach past clients and current contacts.

At Your Event Provide Massive Value

Always under-promise and over-deliver at your seminars and events. The people who attend will be so glad they did because they will receive so much more than they expected. By giving your audience massive value, they now *know* you have massive value to give them. This will make it easy for them to decide to work more with you. They will be inclined to come to more of your seminars or sign up for your group programs or coaching.

Hit All the Bases in Your Program

While you are showcasing yourself and your value, it is also important to include some client examples and the great results your clients have received, so the audience can see themselves in those examples. If you have clients in the room, have them give you a live testimonial. This really helps people feel more confident about working with you, and will increase your sales.

Remember Your "Easy Yes" Offer

Do not forget to invite your seminar attendees to work with you more. Make an offer to have everyone continue to work with you. The goal of each seminar or event is to gain new clients and have people work with you. Just keep delivering massive value to your seminar attendees and they will keep coming back for years to come.

The More Events You Do the Better You Get

I'm sure you see that the more hours you have on the platform the better you become as a speaker. The same is true for doing you own seminars and events. The more you do them, the better you become at doing them, and then you become *masterful* at doing them. When that happens, you will find there is no place you would rather be.

Now you have what you need. Get busy catapulting your speaking business with your own seminars and events. Embrace these strategies and watch your business thrive.

About Caterina Rando

Caterina Rando, MA, MCC, shows women entrepreneurs how to massively monetize their mastery by showcasing their value through speaking and hosting their own events, seminars, and retreats. Join her and women entrepreneurs at the Enliven Summit on *How to Plan, Produce and Profit from a Women's Retreat.*

Caterina also offers a virtual program called *Realize Your Events and Retreats Virtual Action Program.*

Learn more about Caterina Rando at:
CaterinaRando.com/vep

8

⸗Brilliant Advice⸗
from Debbie Saviano

25 Social Media Must Dos for Speakers

On any given day there are over two billion people on social media! Thus, social media should be an integral component of any marketing plan as it helps extend your recognition as a speaker.

These twenty-five tips are based on the philosophy that the goal is to direct clients, potential clients, and interested parties to either a website or a LinkedIn profile.

This is of the greatest importance, as viewers visit both of these in an effort to research and gain information about you. The other social media platforms are primarily focused on the social component, yet they also provide ways you can promote your expertise as a speaker.

Here I give you twenty-five tips for clarity and consistency across social media.

1. *www.about.me*.com is a one-page website where you can share information about yourself, and the best part is how easy it is to use. The site encourages you to include links to other social media sites. For consistency of all the *about.me* pages, each one has a large background image to capture the attention of the visitor.

2. Facebook was the first social media platform and thus, almost everyone has a Facebook account. Facebook is all about being *social*, and so as a speaker, you should be sure to include information in the "About" section noting that you are a *speaker*.

3. Twitter is like a fast moving conversation, and the feed moves quickly. Set up your Twitter bio in such a way that when someone clicks on it, they immediately see you are a *speaker*. It is important to also include your LinkedIn URL in the profile bio (more on LikedIn in 6-22).

4. Google + provides a collation of social and professional content and continues to gain popularity. The primary thing to keep in mind with Google + is that it *is* Google! Therefore, in the "About" section, once again include *speaker* under "Occupation," and also list it in "Skills."

≳ *Brilliant Quick Tip* ≲

Essentially, Google + IS Google, so be sure to state that you are a speaker in the "About" section of your Google + account.

5. Instagram—Up to ninety percent of the information transported to the brain comes from visuals and images. Touch the emotions of the viewer. An Instagram account enables you to show your personal side through pictures that are uploaded. Once again, make sure to include the word *speaker* in the bio portion.

6. LinkedIn is the *professional* social media platform. It's considered *The Golden Virtual Rolodex*. Therefore, utilizing LinkedIn should be considered a *must*!

⋛ *Brilliant Quick Tip* ⋚

Since LinkedIn is the premier social site for professional networking, setting up your LinkedIn profile is a necessity for a speaker.

7. Begin with your LinkedIn *banner* by including images of yourself speaking. Remember, pictures are worth a thousand words, and visuals of you speaking offer subliminal messages.

8. The vast majority of visitors to a LinkedIn profile base their decision to stay or leave on the *headline*. Include the word *speaker* in the headline, and if you want it to stand out, capitalize SPEAKER. Farther down the LinkedIn profile, there will be more space to include details on yourself as a speaker.

9. In "Contact Information," take advantage of the *address* to add the word SPEAKER. Always ask yourself, "*Where are there opportunities to send subliminal messages*?"

10. Continuing in the "Contact Information" section under "Websites," include a simple "Call-to-Action" with this

statement: "Book _____ to SPEAK." LinkedIn allows personalization of the website by adjusting the default to "Other" which opens a third space.

11. In the "Summary" section, include your name, contact information, and the word SPEAKER, so once again, the visitor immediately associates you as a speaker. LinkedIn provides space for 2,000 characters. Use it!

12. Specialties should be included in the "Summary" and in the "Experiences" sections. Under "Specialties," add the word SPEAKER.

13. LinkedIn encourages uploading of images, documents, and resources. Upload your speaker sheet to both the summary section and to your speaker position.

14. Utilize LinkedIn "Experiences" to include SPEAKING. This enables you to have a complete position dedicated to speaking. Include the word SPEAKER in the title and description.

15. Continuing with "Experiences," include your SPEAKING TOPICS in the description. This can be a list of the topics you have spoken on or developed.

16. As a reminder to the viewer, include the phrase, "BOOK _____ to SPEAK" in the description box, and be sure to include the contact information.

17. Remember to utilize the "Add a Link" and/or "Upload a File." If you have a website with a speaker page, include the link, thereby showcasing your skills as a speaker.

18. If you have flyers or images of yourself speaking, upload those in the "Speaker" position.

19. Be sure you have the word SPEAKER in the "Skills" section. Revisit the skills and determine if indeed they speak to your current positions. If not, remove the skills that are not in alignment.

20. The "Interests" provide a way to include your personal interests along with your professional interests. In this case, refer to the *Pareto Principle*—the 80/20 Rule. Interests should be eighty percent personal and twenty percent professional. Consider having a primary interest in capital letters, followed by other interests (ex. ★SPEAKER, LinkedIn, social media, networking). You bring attention to your primary interests with the simple act of capitalizing the word SPEAKER.

⋛ *Brilliant Quick Tip* ⋚

On LinkedIn, under "Interests," eighty percent of those you list should be personal and twenty percent professional. "SPEAKER" should be your primary professional interest.

21. "Advice for Contacting _____ " is the final opportunity on your LinkedIn profile to encourage the visitor to take action. Make sure to add the phrase

"BOOK _____to SPEAK" along with your contact information so you can be reached.

22. Go to the LinkedIn home feed at least once a day and comment on various posts by others. Take advantage of expanding your audience by engaging with those outside your normal daily activity. Be proactive by posting images and quotes, which add value to your skills as a SPEAKER with *influence*.

23. Set up a "Signature" that includes the word SPEAKR, so when communicating in messages and emails, *speaker* will always be visible and assumed—this is considered proactive, yet passive.

24. Social media is about being *social*; it is *not* about selling. If you optimize the space given within each social media platform by adding the word SPEAKER in the bio/profile sections, it will assist with everyone knowing you are a speaker. Remember, "Likes" are what most people give on social media. The real value is in the *comments* and *shares*.

25. Your goal should always be to use social media as a means to *promote, encourage, educate, and engage* with others! The more you are seen on social media, the more *influence* you are perceived to have.

Finally, if your LinkedIn profile is designed strategically, the visitor viewing your profile and seeking information will immediately identify you as a SPEAKER!

About Debbie Saviano

Debbie Saviano spends her time helping other professionals *"Take action and create an online presence"* by developing, nurturing, and maintaining relationships!

With degrees in English, Psychology, and History, and a background in education, Debbie implements a practical approach to social media.

Speaking and training enable Debbie to remain close to those who are interested in learning and embracing technology, and those who seek innovative methods to build relationships.

Debbie started her first career driving a yellow school bus and retired after being a principal of five campuses. Today, Debbie navigates the "virtual highways" and in doing so shows others how to connect, engage, and relate to those they can serve.

Learn more about Debbie Saviano at:
DebbieSaviano.com

9

⋛Brilliant Advice⋚
from Tonya Hofmann

Those Who Make an Impact are Those Who Take Action

This is a book of HUGE ideas for huge thinkers. The very fact
that you are reading it proves you are not only unique and
ready to expand what you know, but that you are ready to
change many lives!

Anyone—but not everyone—can change many lives. The
clear difference is that those who do make an impact are the
ones who take action. That is the *only* difference. Everyone
has learned something, or has an ability that others do not, or
that others would love to have.

Another differentiator of those who make an impact is
that they are quite often a part of a community of like-
minded people. Most people on this planet want to join a
group of others like them, with the same interests, problems,
or challenges.

Taking action and being a part of a community of like-
minded people are what you need to do to make an impact, as
an individual and as a speaker. You can accomplish both!

Ideas of Aires

Millionaires and billionaires have a lot in common. Both
believe in multiple income streams. The difference is that

millionaires have multiple income streams such as real estate, a business, stocks, etc., whereas billionaires have multiple income streams and multiple income streams in every income stream.

I set out in 2007 to figure out how to start thinking like a billionaire. In everything you do, you should ask yourself, *"How can I create another income stream from what I'm doing today?"* Try to create multiple opportunities every time you set out to do something. For example, a *virtual event* not only creates a sale from a client who will be in the event, but you can create sponsors, use it for marketing, invite a guest speaker, gain more exposure, set up revenue share with the guest speaker, and so on . . . get the point?

Personal Growth

"I have one rule I live by now . . .
I'm not allowed to be comfortable!"

-Tonya Hofmann

I realized many moons ago that if I was going to be able to help as many people as possible, that meant I was going to have to get out of all of my fears that had been holding me back my whole life. If you want to help only one person a year, that is much easier than twelve, twenty-four, or twenty-four hundred! I *love* giving back, showing people the possibilities of their world—making a difference, and to me that means helping people beyond my back door. I hired the right life and business coaches who showed me how to think positively, step out of my fears, set goals, accomplish my goals, time manage, network, speak, create a presence on the Internet, and change people's lives. Comfort halts everything. When you are uncomfortable, you are growing.

Imperfection

If you are waiting to make everything perfect, waiting on the time to be perfect, waiting . . . waiting . . . It will never happen.

I started listening to million-dollar-producing speakers and coaches and found that the top people out there have websites with old information, bad grammar, and misspelled words. I listened to their unedited audios and videos, and they made mistakes, said "*Um,*" mispronounced words, said the wrong words, and had all kinds of errors and mistakes, but yet, that didn't keep them from making millions! I figured if they aren't worried about it, why should I be? Sending an imperfect email out to promote an event is better than no email at all. Of course, you should try and correct things but just understand that you have to *take action* or nothing will ever happen!

⋛ *Brilliant Quick Tip* ⋚

Don't wait for everything to be perfect to begin to take action. Do something now!

Funnel Program

The funnel is a simple idea. You pour a whole lot of people in at the top, they filter down until they become fewer people, who become VIP clients. The first level of your funnel is your free area (social media, email campaigns, meeting strangers) and this is the largest group. Every business is different, but most companies have a similar approach. The next level would be the $1 to $50 client. Again, this group is smaller than the free group but larger than the others. The next level would be up to $150 dollars, and so on, until someone gets to your VIP client level for say $5,000 dollars. So the idea is that people come in at the top and slowly filter their way down to the VIP level.

Building a Business

Most small business owners fail to build a business. They offer one or a few services and/or products and they think that is a business. You have to build a foundation and move people through your levels of involvement. I know the funnel works but I think it doesn't work all the time.

I think what really happens is that people come into your business through the courtyard you build. They *love* your courtyard! It's so nice there and, oh . . . it's *free*! The hard part is to get them to be so drawn to your skyscraper (your business), so that they walk inside to the bar area. It's really nice inside and they are so glad they came in to order a drink; however, they finish the drink and you have nothing else to give them to drink so they leave and head back outside. This is called *one-off selling*: you sell them one thing and now they go back to enjoy your courtyard, and it is just as hard to get them to come in again. So, you develop a program that keeps them belly-upped to the bar, and they will never leave. They may take the escalator up to the next floor for dinner, but realistically they love your bar and you can make a whole lot of money there.

I make hundreds of thousands of dollars a year charging $25 to $50 a pop. It is so much easier—people don't have to think real hard about it; they don't have to go ask anyone, and if you get ten people at $50 dollars, that equals $500, which is nothing to sneeze at.

≳ *Brilliant Quick Tip* ≲

Set up your business with various levels that clients can move through, from free, to low cost, to higher cost, to VIP pricing.

Business Groupies

What you should create is *business groupies*! These are the people who hang out at your bar and won't leave. These people are always waiting on the next great thing you have to offer. What is brilliant about this group is that even though they are only buying your lower level products or services, they are incredible testimonials and connections to VIP clients!

No More One-Off Selling

Most entrepreneurs have an incredibly hard time staying in business because every day brings a brand new day they have to go out and hustle to sell again. One-off selling wears out even the hardiest of sales people, and if you don't like sales then it quickly becomes a thorn in your side. So first, you have to ask yourself, *"Which mindset do I have, an employee mindset or an entrepreneur mindset?"* The biggest reason people have a hard time being an entrepreneur is that they can't let go of their employee way of thinking. An employee mindset says, *"I am worth so much per hour. I want to create something once, and it be completed and done. I want to have my next client find me. I want to be paid and then I'm done."*

An Entrepreneur Mindset Says . . .

"I want to constantly tweak everything I create to provide the best value on what my clients want me to provide. I want to constantly be meeting new people even if they don't buy from me immediately, because I know I want them to be in my world forever so that I can continue to change their lives forever, and I will never be done changing their lives which also means I will continue to sell to them."

Which mindset do you have? Are you always looking forward to being done . . . done with your website, done with your current client, done with marketing? So then soon you will be done with business. Every business needs to adjust to the market, which means always adjusting your business.

Easiest Marketing *Ever*

Speaking—even though scary for most—is truly the easiest way to develop yourself and your business! I'll go over the reality and then I'll go over how to get out of your fear of speaking.

Say a new client is worth for you $1,000 a year, and it takes you twenty people to find that one new client. It would take you an entire week, meeting four to six people a day for coffee and lunch, to find that one client. Meetings like this take a long time and cost a lot of money with so many coffees to buy!

Now, let's say you speak in front of group of twenty people who are all potential new clients for you. You speak for one hour and you immediately find your one person out of the group who wants your product or service. You just made your quota in one hour instead of forty hours! And, if you speak just once a month, that's $12,000 a year from gaining just one client per speaking gig.

Fear

I am a recovering introvert so I completely understand how difficult speaking is for most people. You know what? Most people are really nice. I've never had a tomato thrown at me yet. How did I get through the shakes and fainting spells?

Action! I just *did it anyway.* The more I got up to speak, the easier it got. And then one day, I noticed . . . I'm not shaking anymore!

Another thing that would really throw me off was worrying about the negative person in the room who didn't like me. Well, what was there *not* to like? At one speaking engagement, there was a guy who talked to me before the event and he was grumpy and negative. Then, while I was speaking to the group, I saw him shaking his head; he had a grumpy face on, and his arms were crossed. I started my usual panic attack seeing him not "liking" me. Then, I happened to grab a glimpse of a lady to the other side. She was smiling, writing like crazy, and I remembered the great conversation we had beforehand.

Suddenly, it occurred to me that I was focusing on the negative people instead of the positive ones! I also realized something about the people who didn't like me . . . I didn't like them either, so who cares what they think! Twenty percent in a room will immediately not like you, twenty percent will *love* you, and the other sixty percent haven't decided yet.

> ⸞ *Brilliant Quick Tip* ⸟
>
> *Focus on the positive people around you.*
> *Give little attention to the negative*
> *voices around you.*

Own Your Fabulousness

You must showcase how amazing you are because you *are*! Show people you care, that you want to change their lives, and that you're not going any place but up. Don't give up; I'm so glad I didn't. I wanted to several times . . . okay, a *lot* of times, but I didn't. You can't change the world without experiencing the world. I hope you get involved with the *Public Speakers Association*. We love helping make people's dreams come true; showing you the most up-to-date information in the speaking world; giving you a safe environment to practice, tweak, and adjust; and giving you actual opportunities to go change lives from the front of the room!

About Tonya Hofmann

Tonya Hofmann started out in 2005 wanting to change the world but soon realized had to transform herself before she even stepped out of her small community. She went from an extreme introvert who would go through whole days without saying one word to anyone, to now speaking in front of thousands.

Tonya still has the same goal of helping as many people as possible now that she conquered her own stage fright and insecurities. Today, she helps people see their own value, message, and voice. In 2013, Tonya, in partnership with her husband Michael, created the *Public Speakers Association* which is now across the US and Canada. She has her own TV show, is a multi-book author, and has won award after award for being one of the most connected people in the world!

Learn more about Tonya Hofmann at:
TonyaHofmann.com

10

≳Brilliant Advice≲
from Fantastic Frank Johnson

Empower Yourself with Specialized Speaking

First of all, let me congratulate you on your decision to be a motivational speaker. I found fulfillment of my passion in sharing good advice with others.

My specialization began in the field of traumatic brain injury (TBI) and disabled communities. I've used my personal experience and professional coaching to grow the reach of my specialty. I help many people overcome their challenges, whatever they may be. When you decide to specialize in speaking, it will empower you, not encumber you. There is a traditional way of thinking that contends that when you specialize in any profession, you limit your audience and the extent of your reach. I have found the opposite to be true.

Specializing in speaking on TBI, fire safety, and thriving with a disability has enabled me to branch out into many sub-topics. My audience has widened to include, for example, grade-school youth on the topic of fire safety in the home; teenagers on overcoming their challenges to live in their passion; elderly on the topic of following their passion, even in their twilight years; and even job seekers on the topic of raising your expectations to allow yourself possibilities to grow.

> ## ≳ *Brilliant Quick Tip* ≲
>
> *Choosing a specialty in speaking will*
> *empower you, not encumber you. It*
> *opens the doors to many opportunities*
> *and possibilities.*

Step 1: *Find Your Passion*

Define what gives you pleasure in your life. A good example is Billy Graham. He started out as a small town preacher, but when he realized his passion was to run revival events, his public image became well known around the world. My passion became my mission when I realized people with a TBI or other disability needed to know they can thrive *every* day, not just survive day to day.

Step 2: *Label Your Brand*

An example is Simon Jordan. He named his message as "One Planet, One Place." This simple phrase evokes images of peace and unity on Earth that tells the audience his mission, his topic, and his passion. My personal brand is *Fantastic Frank* with the motto *"From Flawed to Fantastic: How to find the Hero in You,"* which is also the title of my first book. Immediately, the audience knows that I am here to help. Taking on the name *Fantastic Frank,* has made me an icon in the United States and with the Brain Injury Association of Canada.

≩ Brilliant Quick Tip ≩

Choose a label for your brand that cues the audience to your mission, your topic, or your passion.

Step 3: *Invent a New Word or Phrase*

Late President Ronald Reagan used his nickname to form a meaningful phrase, "Win one for the Gipper." The American people took this to mean that winning for America was possible in any challenge, especially world politics. I coined the term "differently-abled" to describe that disabled people are still able to do a lot of things, but they may do things differently than they are used to. When you describe yourself as differently-abled instead of dis-abled, you knock people out of their paradigm. I introduce myself like this . . .

"Hi, I am Fantastic Frank,
a differently-abled motivational speaker."

The other person doesn't know what they think about that definition, so they can't put me into a box with a conventional label such as "disabled." The person's mind is open to hearing my story with little to no preconceived bias.

Step 4: *Become an Expert on Your Passion*

While I was earning my college degree in Upstate New York, one of my passions was attending ice hockey games with my friends. I noticed that Clarkson College didn't have a hockey yearbook. They had yearbooks for other sports at Clarkson. They even displayed hockey yearbooks from other New York institutions including Cornell (one of our prominent rivalries).

I learned all I could about the history of hockey at my alma mater. Armed with significant knowledge on players and statistics, I was able to create a hockey yearbook for Clarkson College. I was an expert on my passion. You can also become an expert on your passion.

In step 1, you defined what your true passion is. To become an expert you must find a mentor. This mentor will be someone who has expert knowledge and experience in the topic of your passion. Again I refer to the example of professional sports. Many Americans enjoy football games on television. If this is your passion, then you can contact your favorite team's coach; connect with him; absorb his knowledge in person; or schedule a private telephone interview.

⅊ *Brilliant Quick Tip* ⅊

To become an expert you must find a mentor!

A myriad of other information avenues are available to today's public speaker. The Internet carries a wealth of knowledge and information that seems inexhaustible on any topic. Read all you can find about your specialized topic. Listen to others who have succeeded in public speaking on your specialty. Emulate those people with great influence and advocate for your passionate niche. Once more I say, congratulations on making a huge first step toward personal empowerment by specializing in motivational speaking.

About Fantastic Frank Johnson

Fantastic Frank is an award-winning, dynamic motivational speaker and TV celebrity guest who inspires any audience to overcome and excel at life. One day, while at the height of enjoying success, Frank's life changed forever—he was trapped in a fire, carried out in a body bag, and suffered a Traumatic Brain Injury. He had to re-learn everything, including how to walk and talk. The epitome of perseverance, he turned tragedy to triumph. Frank coined the phrase "differently-abled," and then took his inspiring message to the masses. Now, he appears across America in his signature super hero suit, motivated to inspire millions.

Fantastic Frank is a #1 bestselling author on Amazon, a radio show host, an international speaker, and co-writer of the songs *"A Hero in You"* and *"Being the Change,"* recorded by singer/songwriter Tiamo. His book, *From Flawed to Fantastic*, takes people through a step-by-step process of life transformation.

As an outstanding radio host, he provides hope and help on the Traumatic Brain Injury (TBI) Network. Recognized for his inspirational message, the story "Fantastic Frank" was published in *Chicken Soup for the Soul: Recovering from Traumatic Brain Injury*.

**Learn more about Fantastic Frank Johnson at:
FantasticFrankJohnson.com**

11

≥Brilliant Advice≤
from Candy Barone

Say YES to the Power of Your Authentic Voice:
Strategies to Inspire, Engage & Influence Your Audience

John Quincy Adams once said, *"If your actions inspire others to dream more, learn more, do more, and become more, you are a leader."* I couldn't agree more!

You see, good leaders are trailblazers, people who are able to transform ideas and vision into reality, creating a path for others to follow. Leaders have a voice, a message, and a point of view to share. Leaders instill a belief that something new is possible, that the status quo doesn't have to be. As a speaker, you have the opportunity to lead, to inspire, to engage, and to influence others to take action and create the change you wish to see in the world.

Great leaders, however, inspire their people to reach even higher, dream bigger, go bigger, and achieve more. Great leaders set the stage for others to take greater responsibility and do more with their individual gifts. Leadership is truly the ability to encourage others to see their own greatness, to step into their beautiful light, and to take accountability for the responsibility to share that gift with others. Great leaders help others recognize and leverage their strengths and play to their highest and best value. If you are able to inspire others to reach for the stars, you may find they just might bring you back the moon, as well.

Can you, for a moment, imagine the possibilities available to us and our future generations when we build our teams, our colleagues, our, families, our businesses, and our children in this manner? When we help others see the light within, we unlock the door to their imagination, their creativity, and ultimately, their passion. I don't know about you, but the thought of what truly can be accomplished by great leadership, by each of us (me and *you*) gets me excited and ready to take on this challenge!

So, how does one really become a great leader? It starts by giving yourself permission to say *"Yes"* to yourself first. Ok, what do I mean by this? In order to lead others, you must first learn to lead yourself, from within. Leading yourself starts with being authentic, being genuine, and being courageous to stand in your own light. The person you are outside of work should be the same one that shows up at work! By living intentionally and authentically, you show others how to truly "walk-the-talk." And, how you choose to "walk-the-talk" makes all the difference, and it is a choice—a choice you can make every day in every moment.

It all starts with you finding your authentic voice and stepping into the light that is uniquely yours. You see, the meaning of life is very simple: you were given a song to sing that is yours to sing alone. It may have a similar melody to that of others, but your experiences, your expertise, and your passion create a harmony that is unique and unlike any other. The challenge lies in the question: do you have the courage to step into your light and sing your song loudly and proudly for the world to hear?

Do you realize you were given the most incredible and powerful gift? Again, you were given a song that is only yours to sing! *No one else can sing your song*! Even if some parts of your song may sound similar to another's song, it still has its own music, its own message. No one else can shine the light that is uniquely yours! No one has your exact combination of super powers. This song, this light, is *your* attraction power.

People are attracted to attraction power. You influence and impact people every day without even knowing it. There are people who look to you for guidance, for support, or to be an example for them. You create momentum just by breathing in and out every day. So, why not be more intentional and inspirational in that reality?

So many times I hear those new to the speaking world ask questions like, *"How do I effectively engage with my audience? What is the best way for me to 'show up'? How do I create a message that will resonate with others? How will I know I am delivering value?"* And, there is such beauty in the answers to those questions. As I tell my clients, *"You don't know who, you don't know how, and you don't know to what extent you affect, impact, or influence change for another person, simply by you showing up and being your authentic self. When you add filters, doubt, or the negative self-talk going on in your own head, you take away other's ability to decide how they want to receive you, participate with you, or see value in you."*

When you filter (e.g., say things like "This might sounds stupid" or *"I'm not really an expert"* or *"Who am I to share this"*), you immediately close the conduit of how another person can fully receive you. Their subconscious begins to shut down in response. They say to themselves, *"Well, if they don't believe this is valuable . . . why should I?"* So, rather than engaging, they are distracted, they get shut down, and simply stop listening. You take away their permission to decide and you don't even know you are doing it. The more conscientious you can be in your own awareness about how you present yourself, how you show up, and how you may be inadvertently sabotaging yourself, the more you can open pathways for better and more effective communication. You can provide access for others to learn from you, be inspired by you, and to really engage with you.

₹ *Brilliant Quick Tip* ₹

Let go of the negative self-talk and noise holding you back. Realize you have a song to sing for others that is yours alone. Your purpose is so much bigger than your fear. Walk into your magnificent and empowering light to help others do the same.

You can be the example of what you want others to follow, what greatness you want them to see and live their life in accordance with. You can pay it forward. You can be more courageous and purposeful about the choices you make and what you are setting forth for yourself and others. You can walk-the-talk, live large, and show your truths.

Being able to lead others to greatness is the summation of purpose, passion, and intention working together in a space that inspires and lifts them up. Purpose being what drives you and your business. Passion being what fuels you and why it matters. And, intention being what drives you and creates discipline and accountability.

If you say, *"What difference do I really make?"* you are wasting the very opportunity you were given, the responsibility, and the magnitude of impact that is yours to make. You make a difference, even if you chose to opt out, and that sets an example, too. Not making a decision, or passing the buck, still ends up being a decision . . . and usually one that costs you the opportunity to connect with another person in a way that could serve them or lift them up. It can also cost you the possibility of creating a meaningful relationship that could change your own life. What you want your impact and living legacy in this world to be is up to YOU. It is a choice!

Think about the people in your life who have made a difference to you, whom you have wanted to emulate? Why do they inspire you? What did you learn from them? How might you pay those lessons forward?

Now, think about your own living legacy, what mark do you want to impress upon the people in your life, in your business, in your community, in the world? For every thought and action has a domino or ripple effect in the universe. What you put out now will impact and influence others later. Do you want to inspire that result, or simply let the opportunity to shine your light pass you and others by?

You *do* make a difference and you *do* have a choice in what that difference could be. Choose to inspire, influence, and impact others for greatness! Become an authentic leader and pave the way for others to lead, as well.

For me, that decision came when I chose to leave the security blanket of my corporate career and venture out on my own. I decided that playing small did not serve me . . . nor, does it serve you in any capacity! Because of that fire—that passion that I recognized and acknowledge inside of me—I finally made a conscious choice to take the responsibility that is mine and to live my life with greater purpose and passion, and to use my authentic voice as a tool, as a way to reach and connect with others in order to change the world.

> ⋛ *Brilliant Quick Tip* ⋚
>
> *Challenge yourself every day, in every moment, to step more and more into your light. Acknowledge that playing small doesn't serve you or others either. Know and believe you are a powerful and beautiful child of God. Own it!*

I realized that my purpose—my mission—is to help others find the tools to empower themselves to play bigger. I help people understand the power of learning to destroy the noise holding them back and to empower themselves to believe in what's possible, and to truly let their light shine.

My journey is to help others see how powerful they can be and to be there to guide them through their journey, to break the cycle of fear we continue to pass down from one generation to the next.

Through my work, I challenge people to say Y.E.S. to themselves! In order to say, Y.E.S., I teach others how to be courageous and take a leap of faith now. You Empowered Strong, the name of my company (note the acronym spells YES with purpose), is designed to help others learn how to tell themselves, *"I will stop listening to all the shoulds, all the self-doubt, all the abuse I continue to put on myself . . . and instead, I will change that dialogue to say, 'I can be as powerful as I was designed to be; I am as beautiful and capable as my authentic self; I am strong, empowered, and I choose to share my gifts with others."*

You Empowered Strong was created as a means to break the cycle—a way to empower our youth, our next generation. How do we start teaching them how to give themselves permission, and take responsibility for those choices, *now*, versus waiting until they are forty, fifty, or sixty or more years old, or worse, never? What if our youth learned to play big *now*, to take responsibility for their gifts, and to shine their own unique lights? Can you imagine the possibilities?

It starts with their role models . . . me and *you*! Just think, if we aren't able to give ourselves permission, and demonstrate the ability to empower ourselves for greatness, then how will our children and the next generations to follow learn to do so?

Do you realize that a definitive YES for you means you say NO to all the noise, all the negative self-talk, all the naysayers, all the biased thinking, all the limited beliefs, and all the repetitive cycles we continue to embrace, without ever stopping to ask ourselves, *"Is this my truth*?" and, *"If this is my truth today, do I want it to be my truth tomorrow*? Do I even believe this?"*

You can change that cycle as soon as you decide to change it. The moment you say, *"Enough, I deserve more than this. I believe in the greatness that God put inside of me,"* is the very moment you can step forward into your magnificent light and start to let the leader within you shine.

Yes is a complete sentence, and it is okay—and absolutely necessary—for you to say *"Yes"* to yourself first! The only way you can affect and impact change is to start with yourself. You need to be able to fill your cup before you can give anything to someone else. Learn how to say YES (You Empowered Strong) to yourself.

So, my question to you is, "Are *you ready, truly ready, to step out boldly and let your authentic voice, the leader within you, shine?*" I hope you answered with a resounding YES!

OK then, let's look at some real situations that you might encounter, and the possible strategies you might employ to truly walk-the-talk and create more opportunities to inspire, engage, and influence your audiences. Let's see how one of these situations might show up.

For example, how many times have you walked into a room for a presentation, where you were the keynote or featured speaker, and where you were expecting a big turnout, only to have three people show up? Or, have you ever had one of those times when you were asked to give a talk, was told it was for a small group, only to have many more people show up? More often than not, the former has happened rather than the latter.

Whichever the case, what was your reaction? How did you choose to assess the situation? Did you ever feel like you were thrown off your game in that instance? Were you perhaps, angry, disappointed, intimidated, frustrated, or even unsure of what to do? Maybe you didn't have enough handouts for the size of the group that showed up. Or, maybe the room was so BIG in comparison to the tiny crowd that came to hear your talk. What did you do? How did you react in those situations? Did you see the immense opportunity or did you get frustrated, angry, hurt, and feel like throwing in the towel instead?

Too often I have seen speakers lose their cool in situations such as the one I described. I hear the grumblings, the comments, the frustration . . . statements like: *"This is a waste of my time,"* or *"I cannot believe they didn't get more people to attend,"* or *"How I am going to deliver my message to such a large group—I don't have enough 'stuff' for everyone."* I hear the complaints, the disappointment, the blame, the fear.

But, do you realize that moment is actually a tremendous opportunity? Do you realize everything really is as it is supposed to be? Can you imagine for a moment what would happen if you took hold of the moment and swung for the fences, instead? You see, the audience that *was* supposed to show up did . . . and, in turn, presented you with an opportunity to connect in a real, genuine, and authentic way. For whoever shows up for you, it is up to you to decided whether you will afford them the same respect, the same love, the same level of authenticity. In a single moment, you can decide whether to step up and be the great leader you were intended to be, to shine your light, and to offer something to those who need you, or you can choose to let your own fear, your own insecurities, and your own limited thinking and biases stop you from creating magic and impact.

So, you might be asking yourself, *"How do I turn those instances into opportunities?"* My answer is simple: by believing *they are so.* These moments are your biggest opportunities to build new, meaningful relationships with others, to create conversions for new business, to generate referrals and new leads, and leverage your own strengths and gifts to impact and serve others.

⋛ *Brilliant Quick Tip* ⋜

Keep this mindset: the people who show up for you in your audience are the very people who are supposed to be there for you, regardless of the numbers.

The turning point happens when you make it all about your audience (as it always should be) and get your ego and head out of the equation. *Change your mindset!* You see, by truly saying *"Yes"* to your audience, and ultimately to yourself, you will learn how to inspire, engage, and influence them on a whole new level.

In the end, remember you do not know who, how, or to what level you can impact, affect, or change someone's life just by being you. It is *your* choice as to how you will show up for your audience, no matter the size or who happens to be a part of it. For if you choose to truly say *"Yes"* to your audience and deliver your message in the most authentic way, you *will* see the impact show up in your business. Because, remember . . . nothing happens by accident, and those who showed up did so *for a reason!*

How will you choose to show up in this world? Will you choose to continue to play small, or will you dare to step into your most beautiful and magnificent light? Will you choose to say *"Yes"* to yourself and walk-the-talk to allow others to do the same? Will you let the great and powerful leader within you truly inspire, engage, and influence others for their own greatness?

Remember, the choice is yours to make!

About Candy Barone

Candy Barone, known as the "Pull-No-Punches" accountability powerhouse, is the founder and CEO of You Empowered Strong. She is a Certified Master Coach, a Certified Law of Attraction practitioner, professional speaker, trainer, and author. Candy is a master at helping people say "*YES*" to themselves, destroy the N.O.I.S.E. getting in their way, and create intention and accountability to propel them forward. Candy lives in Austin, Texas, with her puppy, Payton.

Learn more about Candy Barone at:
CandyBaroneInternational.com

12

≷Brilliant Advice≷
from Fred Schuldt

The Power of Our OWN Stories

I was just out of college and had started to work for a large financial services company. It wasn't long before I was exposed to a motivational speaker for the first time. He came across as polished and effective as he shared a story about Spud Webb, who was one of the shortest players in NBA history. The motivational speaker talked about all the obstacles that had to be faced in order for Spud to succeed against all odds. I was motivated and engaged, but at the end I couldn't help but think, *"That was a great story, but I really wish I could have heard Spud Webb tell his own story."* Stories can be powerful, but I sensed instinctively then—and have come to know professionally since as a speaker myself—that the most powerful stories are our own that are shared from the heart.

So why are stories, especially our own stories, so powerful? Storytelling is powerful because it is in our DNA. For thousands of years we have told stories. It started with oral traditions passed down from one generation to the next around the nightly fire. Throughout recorded history, our greatest leaders have been gifted story tellers. We tell stories to communicate new ideas and to inspire change, to engage with others in order to educate, and to warn. We tell stories to find common ground with other tribes or nations or races. We tell stories to celebrate success and most importantly, to emotionally connect. Listening to stories is also in our DNA; because it's something we have always done, it allows us to relax. When settling in to hear a story, we know we don't need to do anything or make any decisions. We also know to pay attention because we have been conditioned to view stories as a way of relaying that which is important.

We remember stories long after we remember facts. Stories have the ability to stop the left brain from seeking more facts and allow the right brain to take the lead. The right brain is the domain for the processing of the "gray areas" in life. The right brain is where we make the decision to trust and ultimately take action based on that trust. The right brain is where we emotionally relate to the human condition. There is great power that comes from sharing stories. That is the power to connect. *And,* the most powerful stories are those that are shared from the heart and where we allow ourselves to be vulnerable. That vulnerability is what connects us on a deeper level with others, and connection is so important in our lives.

⋛ *Brilliant Quick Tip* ⋜

Great power comes from sharing stories.
Stories can stop the left brain from
seeking facts and allow the right brain
to trust, and ultimately take action
based on that trust.

The challenge is that sharing your story from the heart takes getting uncomfortable and being vulnerable. The reason we struggle with being vulnerable is because it means displaying weaknesses and people feel shameful for having weaknesses. Shame is what leads to so much of the bad in our lives.

Shame leads to anger and addiction . . . to abuse and depression. It leads to ALL of the problems we as speakers are trying to help people endure and ultimately overcome. Now here's more good news! Just as *thriving* allows others around you to thrive, when you are vulnerable and share your story from the heart you allow other people to be vulnerable without feeling shame. Because everyone has a story—some inner-struggle—when you pull back the curtain on your life and tell how you overcame the struggles in order to live a fuller more meaningful life, you give people the hope and inspiration they may need to truly look inside and begin their own journey. We all have it in us to get up again and again to turn defeat into victory, so sharing your story from the heart allows others to really look at themselves and say *"Why not me?"*

To do that, you have to share ALL OF IT! When I first decided to start sharing my stories to inspire others, I knew that I had to share it all: the despair, the shame, and the battle to win my life back. If you want to truly connect with an audience you have to reveal ALL of it—the good, the bad and the ugly. Remember, storytelling is in our DNA, so people will instinctually know that something is missing if you hold back.

Also remember that it's not enough to have a great story, you have to be able to connect the dots for your audience. You have to share not only your journey—your story—you have to share what you learned, how you applied what you learned, and most importantly you have to be able to clearly articulate to your audience what it means to *them*. You have to be able to clearly articulate how they can apply what you learned to their own lives to effect change in themselves.

⋛ *Brilliant Quick Tip* ⋚

When you are vulnerable and share your story from the heart you allow other people to be vulnerable without feeling shame.

When I first started sharing my story, it was one-on-one with other young prostate cancer patients. I would tell them about how I had three major intestinal surgeries and prostate cancer between age thirty and forty, hit rock bottom in 2009, and went Heli-skiing in British Columbia, Canada in 2012 to celebrate being cancer free and back on top of the world! Every time I told my story of going from surviving to thriving to someone battling cancer, we would connect *and* people would say *"Wow that's amazing!*

"But . . . how did you do it?" You see it's not enough to inspire and entertain if you want to be truly impactful as a speaker. To truly be impactful you also have to give people tools they can use to make changes, and show them what it means to *them*.

So how do you prepare to share your personal story to connect and turn it into an effective motivational speech that not only inspires people to make changes in their lives, but also gives them the tools they need to effect that change? First you have to get organized, and then you create.

Getting Organized

Step 1

Take some time to start with the end in mind by understanding very clearly who your intended audience is and what your core message will be. This will drive everything else you do.

Step 2

Take your story and break it down into manageable pieces: a list of smaller, three to five-minute stories. You'll want to have as many stories as you can from different parts of your life. This will give you more opportunities to connect with your audience. Some of the stories can be other people's stories but each one should still be personal to you. This may take some time up front, but will make it so much easier later when you are customizing multiple speeches for varied audiences.

Step 3

Give each story a title and define its purpose. Be clear on why you tell this story, what you learned from it, and how that ties in to your core message. Most importantly, each story must have at least one takeaway tool that your intended audience can apply themselves.

Step 4

Review your list of stories and make sure they are all genuine and meaningful. There are many opinions about what makes a great story. For me, when it comes to creating a personal story for sharing in a professional motivational speech, there are four important factors:

1. The story is one you LOVE to tell.

2. The story touches people's emotions in some way.

3. The story creates vivid images in the listeners' minds.

4. The story is perfectly relatable for your audience.

Step 5

Start sharing your stories and the takeaways with people you trust. This will allow you to get feedback so you can refine and improve your stories as needed.

> ⋛ *Brilliant Quick Tip* ⋜
>
> *Break your story down into manageable pieces of three to five-minute stories to use in your speeches. Give each one a title, a purpose, and a takeaway tool.*

Now that you have spent time getting organized and prepared, you are ready to craft your speech.

Whether I'm crafting a sixty-minute key note for a Fortune 500 financial planning firm or a speech for a local charitable organization or school, I use the same repeatable process: *Create-Deliver-Refine*.

Understand Your Audience

In order to *"Create"* your speech you first have to understand as much as you can about your intended audience. This will allow you to tailor each speech to deliver a relevant message they *need* to hear, and one that will satisfy the needs of the organization.

Identify the Core Message

Start with the end in mind. Identify how you will challenge this specific audience by delivering the right call-to-action. I always start with asking two questions. What would a "Home Run" be for me? And most importantly, what is a Home Run for the audience and the organization that *hired* me! Remember that sometimes more is less. If you try to provide too many take-a-ways, if you are too ambitious with your message, it can get diluted. I try to have three to four points I want to really be able to hammer home at the end of each presentation, and one most important call-to-action.

Choose Your Stories

Once I have identified the key points and learnings I need to communicate for any presentation, I simply go back to my list of stories, and choose which stories fit with the core message I need to present and the amount of time I will be presenting. I then put them in an order that makes sense.

At this point I have a working outline. Each story already has a defined reason for being told, a "why it matters for the audience." Each story has a key learning and take-a-way tools for the audience. This approach will ensure that every three to five minutes you are tying your story back to your audience—to why it matters to them. This will also make it easy for you to not come off as scripted, which therefore allows each person in the audience to feel like you are sharing your story from the heart, and with just them. You won't have to memorize a whole script or have a series of slides you look back at to remember where you are. You only need to remember which stories you are telling and why. I end each speech by being very clear on what I hoped they learned from my story and how they can use it to live a fuller, more meaningful life. I do create a few visuals to show at the end of my presentations, when I am recapping what I hoped they learned, so I can hammer home my core message. Besides, some people just need to see it to fully remember, no matter how great your stories are!

Once I *"deliver"* a speech, I gather as much feedback as I can and assess the effectiveness of each story. This enables me to "refine" my message for my next booking, and starts the process all over again.

Being forced to survive three major intestinal surgeries and prostate cancer by age forty, I learned the value of connection. It takes connection to survive. When faced with what seems to be insurmountable challenges, I learned we can't do it alone. And, I learned it's okay to ask for directions, it's okay to get advice. Going on a journey to do more than survive, as a husband and father, youth athletic coach, personal financial advisor, and motivational speaker, I learned it also takes connection to thrive. When you connect from a place of vulnerability, you can be trusted. When you are trusted you can challenge people to take action. When people take action and make changes you have had an impact. When you have an impact on others you can *thrive*. And here's the best part: when you *thrive*, you provide the inspiration and grant the permission needed for others to thrive as well!

About Fred Schuldt

Fred was already considered by some to be an inspirational leader and gifted storyteller, traits that came in handy during his seemingly normal life as a loving family man, successful executive, and coach. But it took the impending loss of that life to truly forge these talents—giving them purpose while giving their bearer perspective. His mission is to arm those around him with the personal skills and inner strength to face adversity before it strikes.

**Learn more about Fred Schuldt at:
Coach-Fred.com**

13

⋛Brilliant Advice⋚
from Elayna Fernández

What Does It Mean to Shine Your Light?

Even though I never thought of myself as a Public Speaker, I can vividly remember how, since my very early years, I was always unconsciously leading and connecting with others through the use of my voice.

My first speech of record was at three years old at my local school. I spoke in front of my class regularly throughout all my school days. I organized my own events as early as twelve years old, and taught *English as a Second Language* at only fifteen years of age.

Thinking myself to be considerably different from any other kids I knew, I didn't always know how I influenced others. I was raised in the Dominican Republic, and at times, we did not have potable water. We had to walk several miles to a small stream with water jugs and buckets. I remember I wasn't strong like my siblings and my friends, so I didn't carry a bucket on my head and one gallon in each hand; I carried a half-gallon but lead the expedition.

When I questioned myself about how helpful I was really being, my father assured me, "*It takes great strength to be a leader and keep your team motivated. You are a wonderful help . . .without you, it would be hard for the group to achieve what they do.*" This was the moment in which I understood the value of leadership and the principle of using the strengths I *do* possess to reach my dreams and bless others.

Ironically, after I moved to the United States, I lacked the confidence to speak to others or speak in public, which meant I did not use my gift of leadership.

As a speaker, you are a leader with a sacred responsibility because words create. As you stand on the stage, you are creating *influence*, *income*, and *impact*, which I consider to be the ingredients of *legacy*.

In late 2004, I was faced with a moment of great uncertainty that led me to start a business. For a few years, I was comfortable hiding behind HTML codes and guerrilla marketing strategies. As my business grew and the word spread out, I was invited to teach web design classes, email marketing, blogging, and social media classes. Being a successful entrepreneur gave me the time, freedom, and flexibility to influence my daughters; it also provided the financial means I needed as a single mom to provide for my family, and it made an impact on those who needed my services to grow their own influence, income, and impact. When we use our gifts to bless others, we create a ripple effect of miracles.

In January of 2009, because of the release of the *Beyond the Secret* movie, I became acquainted with Les Brown, one of the world's most renowned speakers, and decided to go to a convention in Las Vegas, specifically with the goal to meet him.

I loved his speech, and while everyone was absorbed in a standing ovation, I ran through security like a Dominican baseball player and went backstage, with five-inch heels! I felt this was my chance and nothing was going to stop me. Security caught up with me but by that time I was hugging Les and giving him my business card. Les asked the security guard to take a picture of us. I chuckle just thinking about it.

Back home, I couldn't stop talking and blogging about how I met Les Brown. About ten days after the event, I received a phone call and the caller identified himself as Les Brown. I was convinced it was a prank call, but as it turns out it wasn't. I was officially invited to join his team as a Webmaster and Brand Strategist.

Having the opportunity to work with and develop a friendship with Les and many of the influential people he called friends and colleagues, opened my eyes to how adding public speaking to your marketing plan really can skyrocket your results. I loved learning the secrets of highly successful, internationally acclaimed, and sought-after speakers. Most importantly, I decided to embrace my gifts once again, which started an unfolding manifestation of my destiny. Les' friendship has been a blessing to me, of which he says, "*You made it happen, Elayna. Out of 3,000 attendees, you ran backstage . . . YOU were HUNGRY!*"

"*You Gotta Be Hungry!*" is his signature phrase, a very important component to his brand that springs out of his story. He went from being born in an abandoned building in Liberty City, FL, eating scraps from families for whom his adoptive mother worked as a maid, and being labeled "the dumb twin," to three-term state legislator in Ohio and winner of The Golden Gavel Award as a keynote speaker, bestselling author, and speaker/trainer and coach.

What started as a great opportunity to grow my web marketing business, turned into an exciting opportunity to share my story with millions of people worldwide and live my true calling.

What Does it Take to Become a BRILLIANT Speaker?

Believe it or not, my name—Elayna—is of French origin and it literally means "brilliant," "sun ray," and "shining light." I have learned that to be brilliant means to be confident, to share your gifts, and to bless others with your works.

> *Ye are the light of the world. A city that is set on an hill cannot be hid.*
>
> *Neither do men light a candle, and put it under a bushel, but on a candlestick; and it giveth light unto all that are in the house.*
>
> *Let your light so shine before men, that they may see your good works , and glorify your Father which is in heaven (Mathew 5:14-16, KJV).*

I love acronyms, so I created one just for you, to illustrate how you can become a B R I L L I A N T speaker.

Be You!

Many coaches will tell you to practice and memorize a speech. While preparation is a required principle to succeed in any endeavor, being yourself is essential if you want to leave a lasting impression on your audience. You must let your passion shine, which is why you must discover your passions so your speech will reflect that the topic is meaningful to you and that it is part of the overall contribution you want to leave as a legacy.

Being *you* requires you to be authentic, open, and flexible. Before you go out and speak, commit to speak from the heart, focus on what matters, and be intentional about the difference you want to make.

Research Your Audience

Do your homework and find out who your audience will be.

> ⋛ Who are they?

> ⋛ What do they most desire or dream about?

> ⋛ What problems or questions keep them up at night?

> ⋛ What are their fears?

> ⋛ What really matters to them?

⋛ *Brilliant Quick Tip* ⋚

Get to the bottom of how you can add value to your audience. Discover what really matters most to them.

I usually speak at conferences for mom bloggers and I really love that we have a forum where we connect before, during, and after the event. This presents an opportunity to connect with them and truly get to the bottom of how I can add value to their lives. I guarantee if you do the same, you will be pleasantly surprised as to how important this step will prove to be in your effectiveness as a speaker.

An exercise you can do right now is to imagine the person you want to serve, and write a description of who they are and for what they are asking seeking and knocking. Here's a description of the mom I want to serve:

> The woman I serve is a mom blogger who is overworked, overwhelmed, and overloaded with her roles as a mom, wife/homemaker, and woman, and she wonders if there is a way to balance it all without losing her sanity. She is ready to create the extraordinary life she dreams of. She wants to find her purpose, pursue her dreams, and live her passion.
>
> She often finds herself discouraged, devastated, doubtful, and depleted by her painful reality. Feeling lost and alone in her journey, she deeply wants support, tools, resources, and encouragement to feel like she can make it through the physical, emotional, spiritual, financial, and relationship hardships, trials, and challenges she faces in the everyday chaos.
>
> While she strives to be a guide, a mentor, and a nurturing catalyst for her children, she struggles with low self esteem: feeling inadequate, guilty, ashamed, unqualified, or simply "not enough." She needs to discover her greatness, her divine purpose, and her inner power. She needs the hope that can only be found in inspiration from another woman who has made it through.

Invite the Spirit

When you walk on stage, be quiet for a few seconds, take a deep breath, center yourself, and summon the courage to share what serves the audience.

When you're a mom, you can actually choose to be a child again. I just recently learned to swim and to ride a bike with my daughters. While it was an exhilarating experience and quite an achievement—because I'd been waiting for decades to learn—it started out as a source of fear. After my first lesson, I wrote a blog post about three powerful ways to conquer your fear that I feel also apply to public speaking:

1. Choose to be excited

2. Choose to trust

3. Choose to follow baby steps without judging yourself harshly

Choose to know that you are not nervous; you're just excited about the inspiration, information, and invitations you are about to share. The feelings we experience when our body communicates fear are often the same ones we feel upon the anticipation of something amazing that is about to happen.

৩ *Brilliant Quick Tip* ৼ

Simply decide not to be nervous. Think of your feelings as anticipation of something good that's about to unfold.

Trust and allow God to speak through you. When you invite His Spirit to join the conversation, your words suddenly become more powerful and you develop a greater capacity to touch the lives of those who desperately need breakthroughs, guidance, and change.

Don't judge yourself harshly or—at all. If you are in business, you already know to be professional and hone your craft, but focus on the message, not on the messenger. It's not about you, after all; it's all about those for whom the message is intended.

Love Your Audience

Jesus Christ was unarguably the best teacher, speaker, and master who ever walked on Earth—or water, for that matter. He spoke simply, used unrefined analogies, and shared proven blueprints to achieve massive results without having to call them that.

I believe that what made him so incredibly commanding, compelling, and influential was His amazing love for each individual He spoke with and taught. I invite you get clear on your audience and to fall in love with them. Ask yourself these questions:

- ⸗ Do you love those with whom you share your wisdom, your knowledge, and your expertise?

- ⸗ Are you passionate about helping them find solutions to their problems and achieve their goals?

- ⸗ Are you fulfilled by the impact you can make in each of their lives?

When you love your audience, you can bless them, and you will be blessed!

Listen to Your Audience

The most inspiring, engaging, and entertaining speakers know that a valuable presentation is a conversation with the audience.

There are many simple ways you can interact with the audience: asking them to raise their hand, to stand up, to say something to one another, to close their eyes and visualize a scenario, to write down or tweet a particular phrase, or to follow along with a hand out.

In most cases, I prefer questions and answers (Q&A) after I have delivered my presentation; it is more effective for me to stay on track while providing the value I am committed to give. However, it is sometimes appropriate to ask someone in the audience a simple question, preferably a closed question (with a yes, no, or simple answer) or to call someone to the stage for a demonstration.

In any case, make it a habit to notice how people react to what you are teaching. Study their body language, and let them know you care.

When you come across the person who is shaking their head, frowning their face, raising their eyebrows, or saying something to disrupt the flow, just ignore them and focus on those who value your message—you are there to serve them, exclusively.

Inspire Action

For most speakers, a call-to-action involves sales or conversion. Don't get me wrong, I get paid to speak, and my speaking engagements do grow my business and profits; however, I choose not to resort to blatant pitching, shameless self-promotion, or to using methods of pressure to get people to buy, sign up for, or download something.

Inspiring action means giving your audience something valuable and inviting them to implement what they learn.

- ⋛ You can give your audience information on how to dig deeper, how to learn more, or simply take the next logical steps toward their desired goal.

- ⋛ You can make them aware of tools they can use to get closer to their dream or make it easier to achieve it.

- ⋛ You can give them more access to you.

There are certainly many ways you can inspire your audience to take action, just make sure they serve your audience and it truly fulfills a need.

Aim for Genuine Emotional Connection

Something that really helped me when I was starting out as a speaker was to write my story and get crystal clear about exactly how I wanted my story to affect my audience. I wrote it down and made it concise, leaving out the fluff, and focusing on which parts helped me express feelings that were familiar to them.

Speaking is a great way to leverage your knowledge, your wisdom, and your expertise, but this doesn't mean you need to "talk to a crowd" in the literal sense.

Instead of scanning the room, when I am on the stage or in any teaching setting, I like to consciously lock eyes with individuals throughout the lesson or speech. It may sound counter-intuitive, but actually, it is kind of magical: the whole audience becomes engaged and affected by this connection.

≷ *Brilliant Quick Tip* ≷

Instead of scanning the room with your eyes during a speech, make eye contact with various individuals throughout the room, which can work beautifully to engage your audience.

I must say that the most emotional setting I've experienced was during Anthony Robbins' *Unleash the Power Within* seminar. And even Oprah agrees! I truly enjoyed walking on hot coals and feeling almost invincible, but there was more: it was the collage of emotions that I felt that made it unforgettable, life-changing, and real.

Robbins' top tip for succeeding as a speaker: " . . . *and the way to move an audience is by becoming moved yourself, which can only happen if you're being genuine. Make it real and raw* . . . "

Name Specific Solutions

Name specific solutions to their problems and answers to their questions. I've come up with a simple *Signature Speech Formula* that can remind you about what the essentials are when you are sharing your presentation with an audience:

Statistics
+ Story
+ Solutions
_____
= Signature Speech

There are many more elements you can add, of course, but these are the basics to let your audience know you have done your homework; they can relate to you; and you care about them and are there to give, not to take.

It's plain and simple, as stated by Theodore Roosevelt (and Zig Ziglar, and many others), *"People don't care how much you know, until they know how much you care!"*

Thank Them

I have spoken at a lot of events, and shared the stage with many speakers—both beginners and seasoned masters. One big mistake I've seen is that some don't take the time to thank the audience.

Thank the audience for their time, for their attention, for their applause. One of my favorite proverbs (original author unknown) says, *"The best gift someone can offer you is their time, because it is something they will never get back."*

While we are in gratitude mode, remember to thank the event promoters, the event sponsors and exhibitors, and the support staff or volunteers, when appropriate. Gratitude is a virtue that truly breeds success.

The Business of Speaking

Now that you know my secrets to being a B R I L L I A N T speaker, how I strive to live up to my namesake, and some ways you can get started, let's go on to talk about profits. Income is an equally important part of the legacy trifecta that I mentor moms to pursue.

As a Guerrilla Marketing Master Trainer, I focus on profits as the yardstick to measure marketing. Something I have learned from working, collaborating, and sharing the stage with some of the most distinguished speakers in many arenas is that they all know how to market themselves and have a balance between the heart of public speaking and the business of public speaking.

I came up with a formula that you can use to start profiting from your ability to speak:

$$\frac{\begin{array}{l} \textbf{Credibility} \\ +\ \textbf{Vulnerability} \\ +\ \textbf{Visibility} \end{array}}{=\ \textbf{Profitability}}$$

Credibility and vulnerability as a speaker come from following the *Signature Speech Formula* I shared before, but how do you increase your visibility?

When I teach about marketing, I break down the process into five stages, because through my personal journey helping moms position themselves to make six-figures from home so they can enjoy time with their children, I have learned that contact and exposure is necessary—but not enough—to brand yourself as the solution to your target market's problems.

Visibility goes beyond exposure, because it's not "getting seen," but "*what you get seen as*," that counts.

The 5 Stages of the Marketing Process

1. *Contact* is the first step of the process. Most of us are great at his, and we call it networking or social networking.

2. *Conversation,* according to Wikipedia, is "*a form of interactive, spontaneous communication between two*

or more people." By listening to your audience, as we have discussed, you can deliver what is relevant to their needs, wants, and desires.

3. *Connection* is imperative so you can create deep and lasting bonds.

4. *Community* refers to "*a social unit of any size that shares common values*," according to Wikipedia. It takes twenty-seven exposures before someone decides to buy from you, so you must develop a way to keep the conversation going.

5. *Conversion*, according to Merriam-Webster, is "*the process of being converted.*" Conversion is a change of heart that we cannot "make happen." We can only facilitate it. Conversion refers to lasting transformation.

If you look at the words *conversion* and *conversation*, the difference is the letters AT. Because I'm a word-nerd, I can clearly see that in order to get others on board with our product, service, or ideas, we must stop speaking AT people and start conversing *with* them. Like I often say, "*The only way to convert is to converse.*"

Are you having a conversation with your audience that leads them to connect so deeply they become converted?

I am very grateful for your time and for the conversation we have shared through Margo's brilliant facilitation. It is my prayer that you take these principles to heart so you can have the influence, income, and impact that create JOY, BALANCE, and lasting SUCCESS . . . on your own terms. God bless you!

BE Positive and You'll BE Powerful!

About Elayna Fernández

Elayna Fernández, The Positive MOM, is a vegan Latina homeschooling mom of all girls, living in Texas. As a best-selling author, international keynote speaker, and award-winning mompreneur, Elayna teaches moms how to turn their pain into their purpose and their passion into their paycheck so they can create JOY, BALANCE, and SUCCESS on their own terms and without the guilt, struggles, and overwhelm. Elayna blogs at ThePositiveMOM.com, where she pours her heart out about the topics of motherhood, mompreneurship, and motivation for moms. Elayna considers herself a geekess and word-nerd and her philosophy is, *"BE Positive and You'll BE Powerful!"*

Learn more about Elayna Fernández at:
ThePositiveMom.com

14

⸾Brilliant Advice⸾
from Ha Tran

Stage Presence and Strategies

Giving a memorable speech does not just happen when you step in front of an audience. If all you do is go stand in front of an audience and speak without any kind of preparation, your chances for success are very small. The art of effective speech-making starts long before the actual event.

Preparation is the secret to your success. Perhaps you think this is not such a big secret—you know you must prepare. Still, many, many speeches fail because of the lack of adequate, solid preparation. The speech fails because the preparation failed.

Perhaps you think that there must be secrets to adequate preparation. But there really are no secrets, just solid, proven techniques that you either don't know or have overlooked.

So, what are the critical aspects of good preparation that you must consider? How do you avoid failing to give a great speech by not failing to do a great job with preparation?

In this chapter you will find the answers to that question. Good preparation is paying attention to basics: research your material, script out your speech and put your talk on paper, dialogue (practice out loud) your lines repeatedly, practice the wording with someone who can critique you well, work on using words that are clear and enhance your delivery, practice your facial expressions in the mirror, work on having gestures that demonstrate and emphasize your points, understand your speaking style and how you deal with stress, and develop a pre-talk routine to be ready to give your best performance.

The more pre-work, i.e., preparation you do, the better your delivery will be. Take the time to prepare and both you and your audience will be thrilled by what a wonderful speaker you are!

Preparing For Your Presentation

When you are preparing for a speaking engagement there are important questions you must answer in order to maximize your success (in addition to using a questionnaire, as a part of your Event Planner):

1. What is the title of your program? (Give your story a memorable name and file it for future use.)

2. What is the message you want the audience to go home with?

3. What personal or professional struggles will you share with your audience?

4. What is the make-up of the audience:

   - Number of attendees
   - Age group
   - Gender
   - Socioeconomic status
   - Other characteristics relevant to your topic

5. When will you speak, i.e., morning, evening, breakfast meeting, luncheon, etc. If you are part of a panel, what is your position?

6. Will there be other speakers on the platform?

7. What is the seating arrangement for the audience, and where will you be positioned in relation to the audience?

8. Are there any topics that are off limits?

9. Will you need any audio-visual aids: projector, screen, etc.? Don't forget a microphone!

10. Will you be selling any back-of-the-room products, such as a book, CD, or signing people up for a program? Do you have the organizer's permission to do this? Do you have a table for the products, and someone to help sell, take money, gather names for your mailing list, etc.?

11. Make sure you get a list of the names, phone numbers, and email addresses of the people who have scheduled you and who may also know your audience, so you can contact them and get acquainted.

Preparing the Presentation

How you present your information makes a huge difference in your effectiveness as a speaker.

One of the most important things to be aware of is that all people have one of three different learning styles (or a combination, but one is usually dominant). Understanding these styles and couching your information in terms that get through to each of these learning styles will help you reach as much of your audience as possible.

These learning methods are *Visual, Auditory,* and *Kinesthetic* (movement)—VAK for short. These are the three main sensory receivers by which people take in information and that determine each person's dominant learning style. Each learning modality receives information differently, so putting your information into three different versions will ensure maximum comprehension.

Keep these three in mind as you prepare your actual presentation—your speech or talk.

Your Actual Talk or Presentation

At its most basic, a talk has three parts. (Remember your basic high-school or college essay? It's the same principle!) The three parts of a speech: The *Introduction, Body,* and *Conclusion*.

Introduction

A strong opening statement attracts your audience and draws them into the rest of your speech. It establishes your credibility and answers for your listeners the question *"What's in it for me?"* It tells them the benefits of listening to you.

It is crucial to let your audience know what you will be covering in your talk at the very beginning, so they know what to expect. Be sure to do this within the first two paragraphs of your introduction.

Even if you will be speaking from notes, your introduction is very important and should be memorized.

> ## ﹥ *Brilliant Quick Tip* ﹤
>
> *Within the first few phrases of your introduction, let your audience know what you will be covering in your talk so they know what to expect.*

Body

The body is the main part of your speech and should contain the three or four points you want to make. Each point should be about ten minutes.

More points than three or four usually are a mistake. If you make too many points, the audience will not remember them and will forget most of what you said. If you squeeze too much in, you squeeze the audience out.

You must also build in pauses to let your audience laugh or think, and let what you have said sink in.

Be sure to adapt the body of your speech to the individual needs of your audience and make it personal to the group you are speaking to.

Conclusion

This is just as important as your introduction and should also be memorized. This is the last chance for your audience to remember your words of wisdom.

Never end your speech with a question and answer session (Q&A). This can lead to far too many unknowns and ruin everything you have said. It is important that you have the last word and that the last word be clear!

Make a strong closing statement. What sticks with people is generally the last thing they hear, so consider your closing statement very carefully.

If you are going to do a Q&A session, be sure to end your talk with your strong closing statement, and pause for a few minutes to let it sink in. Then you can open the floor to questions.

Making Your Presentation the Best it Can Be

Giving a great speech is not just putting your points down on paper and then reciting them. There are many things you can do to make your presentation clear, powerful, memorable, and generally a hit. Take the following considerations into account and use them to make your talk the best it can be.

Clarity

Know your intended outcome; in other words, what message you want the audience to go home with? Do you want them to be inspired? Do you have a particular action you want them to take? Do you want them to have a particular knowledge set they can use?

Determine this at the beginning of writing your speech, as it will both make your writing clearer and make it easier to be sure you have gotten your message across clearly.

You must tell your audience clearly at the beginning of your speech what your message is and in what direction your speech will go. If you are not clear the audience will not be clear and will make a decision to tune you out within thirty seconds of the start of your talk. So it bears repeating, be very clear about your message and the intended outcome of your talk.

Stories

One of the best ways to catch and hold your audience's interest, as well as convey important information, is to tell a story. The ability to tell a great story is a very important skill that makes a great impact on your audience. Tell a good story and make a good point.

A great story is extremely powerful and there are two reasons why. First of all, if you choose to share your personal story, it is absolutely unique and has only happened to you and therefore is something only you can share. The second reason that stories are powerful is because all humans have the same emotions. Stories build on and use the emotions we all possess. Sharing stories allows the audience to be a part of your message and share commonality with you.

In order for your story to have maximum impact, work on your story development before you stand up to speak. Write your story lines out long hand. Practice "talking" on paper.

This kind of pre-rehearsal will breathe life into your story when you tell it in your speech.

Remember that your speech is a journey—a journey where your intention is to bring your audience along with you.

≥ *Brilliant Quick Tip* ≤

Think of your speech as a journey where you bring your audience with you from a clear starting place to an expected end.

145

This is a technique for telling a great story and it consists of six steps:

1. **Structure:** make sure you have a timeline in place for structuring your story, even if you will be jumping around. Be sure to move from one time or event to the next in the proper progression.

2. **Set the scene.** What is going on at the beginning? Paint a background for your story to make it more colorful to your listeners.

3. **Introduce your characters.** People relate to people. Limit the number of people in the story to three. This will help the story be clearer and will create more understanding of your tale.

4. **Encounter some obstacles and challenges.** Put adversity into your story. Knowing that you understand real-life problems will make your speech more believable.

5. **Resolve the story's problem.** Don't leave the listener wanting to know more. Solve the hurdles for them and let that be your point: you are offering solutions that overcome difficulty.

6. **How does the story end?** Make your point. Pull the audience in by showing them that the resolution of the story's problem can influence their reality. Pause and give your audience time to reflect on how the story offers insights and solutions for dealing with their own life's challenges. And most

importantly, offer encouragement that they can overcome their difficulties.

Final words about story telling: Lou Heckler said, *"Don't tell your story, relive it."* In other words, put your emotions into the storytelling so the audience can experience it through you. You will find that has a very powerful impact.

My mentor, Dr. Kenneth Crannell, gave me a great tip: Think the thought before you say it. Otherwise, it just sounds like babble. Impression precedes expression.

Pauses

"Pause instead of pose, it will show poise" (author unknown). Toastmasters and professional speakers claim this tip that is one of most powerful and effective tools in speaking. There are a number of reasons that a pause is effective; however, I would just like to mention four reasons for using a pause:

1. It gives the audience time to reflect on their own lives and how the talk affects them.

2. It gives the audience time to catch up with you and digest the information you just presented to them.

3. It adds impact to an important statement or significant point.

4. Pause after humor: this lets your audience laugh. Do not step on their moment of fun!

Humor

There is the story of a new and inexperienced speaker who attended his first National Speakers Association meeting. He asked an old pro, *"Do I need to use humor?"* The old pro answered wisely, *"Only if you want to get paid."*

Humor is a very powerful tool to interject life and emotion into your story. It is not easy to be naturally humorous, so your style of humor should be an extension of your personality and be natural. It sometimes takes years to successfully develop stage humor.

If you are uncomfortable with this tool don't use it, at least while you are starting out as a professional speaker. Like anything else, humor is a skill that can be learned.

One kind of humor a successful speaker will use is self-deprecating humor. You poke fun at yourself and share your failures and faults. This humanizes you to the audience and immediately makes you more likeable. Remember, you must connect with your audience before you persuade.

Use Dialogue Rather Than Narration

Too many speakers employ narration rather than dialogue, which is less effective. Rather than telling the audience what a character says in your story, have the character himself or herself speak, act, and show emotion. This technique will make your speech a live, dramatic event and paint a strong picture.

Less is more in this practice. Dialogue takes less time and is very effective in making points clear. For example, instead of saying, *"I went home and told my parents that I wanted to drop out of college and travel to find myself. To which they responded with surprise and amazement."*

Use dialogue instead: *"I told my parents 'Mom and Dad, I want to drop out of college and go out in the world and find myself!' They said 'What? Are you out of your mind? We are not going to support you so you can "find yourself"* [use air quotes]!'"* This shows the change in emotion from excitement to disappointment and it shows the real reaction of mom and dad in literal action.

Choreography

Choreography is the plan of your movements on the stage, where you stand and position yourself for different parts of your talk. It is using stage space in the most effective manner for your talk.

Stage space is the most valuable real estate a performer has. Standing still is a waste of this space.

Therefore, a dynamic speaker uses their stage well to showcase their message. To do this, be aware of the audiences perspective, which is left to right. You, as the speaker on the stage, move right to left to match to the audience's perspective.

There are three reasons to incorporate movement into your speaking:

1. It creates a timeline. The past is to their left (which is your right), the present is the middle stage, and the future is to their right (your left).

2. It creates movement in your story. The characters move deliberately and you demonstrate this in movement.

3. To position different characters in your story with different locations. This will create memory retention.

Practice, Practice, Practice

Now that you have written your speech and figured out what your stage movements are, it is time to *practice.*

It cannot be emphasized enough that you need to practice in front of real people. Speak to anyone who will listen. Grab a child, a spouse, a friend, a neighbor, and have them listen to your talk. Ask them to give you honest feedback. Use what they have told you to improve your speech and your performance.

Also, practice in front of a mirror. You need to see what you look like when you speak and you need to practice your choreography.

Actual stage time is a very important preparatory tool. Talk when you can and never turn down an offer to take the stage.

The goal should always be to make the stage your own. If you are comfortable, it will be much easier to captivate your audience. The reward will be the satisfaction of being asked to come back to speak again or of gaining a referral to the group's extended network.

Attitude and Mindsets

Have the right attitude and mindset when you are going to speak. This begins even before your audience walks into the room. Tell yourself positive things about your ability to speak and how great your performance will be. Have some positive affirmations you can say to get yourself into an upbeat, confident, positive mood.

Say to yourself, "*I love my audience. I love my audience. I love my audience.*" Then make it your purpose to show them how much you love them.

Meet and greet your audience as they arrive. Position yourself to speak to them as they enter the meeting room. Relax, enjoy and appreciate that moment of acquaintance.

Remember these people came to see and hear you!

Make it a point to remove all the obstacles between you and your audience, such as a lectern, table, or chair (unless you really need them). This gives your audience the message that you are open and available to them and really care about them.

Have an attitude of enjoyment in your speaking, it will come across to the audience and help them like you and be open to your message.

Expect the Unexpected

Be aware that things can change in a minute, or at the last minute.

A mentor told me I must be ready for anything. The T-shirt philosophy "stuff happens" proves to be true. Expect the unexpected.

Quite a few times I have been told to cut my presentation short because someone else who went before me exceeded their allotted time. One time, the director of an event asked me to speak for forty-five minutes. At the last minute she asked me to cut my talk down to twenty minutes because she had just discovered that her staff wanted to use the occasion to surprise her for her birthday. Don't let something like this shake you!

As part of your good-practice, advance preparation, make sure to have a shorter version of your speech available. This will be a version that still accomplishes your target but uses fewer of your points in the body of your speech. By being prepared you will be able to give a graceful, coherent speech and no one will know that you had to cut it short.

⋛ *Brilliant Quick Tip* ⋚

Have a shorter version of your speech ready in case you are asked at the last minute to cut your presentation short.

Just Before Your Presentation

What you do an hour before your presentation is crucial. Just as you wouldn't drink caffeine before going to bed because it is counterproductive to good sleep, there are productive and counterproductive things to do just before you speak.

Avoid eating before your presentation for at least an hour or so. The time and energy needed to digest your food can take away from your best performance. Therefore, if you are speaking at a breakfast meeting or another meal, it is best to eat beforehand.

Different speakers have different rituals that they do. Some meditate. Some pray. Some exercise their jaw; some do tongue exercises; some do push-ups. There are as many different preparatory exercises as there are speakers. But the key is to find what works for you to maximize your readiness to speak and energizes you towards a maximum speaking performance. Therefore, experiment with what gets you in the right condition and mindset to speak powerfully.

Your Stage Presentation

Now, you are ready for your stage presentation. You have completed the initial steps to owning the stage. You have a positive mindset and you have made strategic partners out of your audience, instead of having them be just a group of unknown strangers.

The time has come to perform. Have fun. Relax. Take it easy. Let your preparation translate into confidence.

Are you a little nervous? Of course you are. But now is the time to triumph. Now is the time to turn this nervous anxiety into a positive energy that energizes and improves your talk.

Remember that you love your audience. Remember that you have an important mission and a great message to share. If you do it right, you will change the way they think and ultimately the way they act. In so doing, you will change their lives for the good. So, be poised in your assurance. Be sure of yourself in this, the moment of performance. It is your time to shine!

Following are the techniques that professional speakers use to own the stage.

The YOU Factor

YOU is the most important word in your speech. You as a speaker must be focused on your listeners. Your audience is what the event is all about: they are the "you" for whom you are there. Everything must be focused towards them. You want them to feel important and your actions must convey that to them.

Your audience is the center of your focus. Let go of your ego. The presentation is not about what you think; it is what you *know* that will benefit them. It is a time to give. It is a time to be centered around the needs of those to whom you speak.

Engage the Audience

Involve the audience in your talk and get them to participate in your presentation. There are many ways to engage your audience:

1. Ask/raise questions to the audience, such as, *"Have you ever?"* or *"How about you?"* and then allow time for replies.

2. Use statements that invite the audience to participate, such as *"Imagine . . ."* or *"I wish you were there . . ."* or *"Picture yourself . . ."*

3. Play games with the audience; adults love to play games. It brings back yester-years and youthful times. It brings a fun element to the talk.

4. Ask for help with something. Have a volunteer help you make a point.

Make sure when you ask questions of the audience, that they are important, purposeful questions. Instead of asking, *"How many of you have been to Boston?"* personalize the question and ask, *"Have you ever been to Boston?"*

Be specific, because being specific makes things more memorable. Make your personal stories very detailed. Do not generalize the events but use relatable, clearly-described details. Make it a point to utilize pleasant sounding words, colorful words, descriptive words, and explosive words.

Okay. It is time for you to do what only you can do: give a presentation that is unique to you! Start presenting and stop worrying. Remember that you are aligned with your strategic partner, your audience.

About Ha Tran

Ha Tran is the author of *Empowered by Hope* and co-author of *25 Brilliant Business Mentors*, a best seller on Amazon.com.

Ha is a successful entrepreneur, Life/Business/Sales Coach, wife and mother.

Ha is a member of the Les brown Platinum Speaker Network, and a Certified Diamond Public Speaker Mastery member of Eric Lofholm International Inc.

Today Ha is a successful business woman and a gifted communicator who touches audiences with her inspirational story of professional and personal triumph.

Learn more about Ha Tran at:
HaTranSpeaks.com

15

⋛Brilliant Advice⋜
from Susan Tolles

4 Pitfalls to Becoming a Phenomenal Speaker

If you had told me a few years ago that public speaking would be part of my future, I would have laughed! I'd had a real "trial by fire" with my first speaking engagements, giving graduation speeches for five years to audiences of up to 3,000 people as a school board president. To say I was terrified would be an understatement. When I left that role, I gladly left the speaking requirements behind.

As I moved on, I transferred my passion for excellence from the education realm to something much different—midlife women. As a woman over fifty who was at a major crossroads in life, I followed my intuition, took a giant step out of my comfort zone, and founded Flourish Over 50, a lifestyle website to inform and motivate women in life after fifty. As that endeavor matured, I came out from behind the computer and grew into my authentic self with a much larger vision. My passion for inspiring women has led me to something I never would have dreamed I'd embrace: public speaking.

Why is this so different now? Why am I actually enjoying getting in front of people to share my message, instead of dreading the experience? Primarily, it is part of my life purpose, to inspire and equip women to flourish from the inside out. There is no better way to play big and use my gifts to their fullest potential than by speaking at conferences, retreats and workshops.

I also now recognize four major pitfalls to becoming a great speaker, and have learned how to avoid them as I have become more confident in this role. In sharing these four pitfalls with you today, I hope to inspire and equip you, too, as you become the phenomenal speaker you are destined to be.

Pitfall #1: *Perfectionism*

Perfectionism can be the secret to your success, or the saboteur of your sanity. It can be a healthy motivator to achieve more, produce higher quality work, and approach every speech striving for excellence. But when it becomes an obsession, it can wreak havoc on your personal life and career, causing stress, exhaustion, and disappointment. Believing that you must look perfect, have a perfect speech delivery, create a perfect website, and present a perfectly written speech for people to like you can lead to "speaker paralysis," keeping you stuck in neutral instead of sharing your gifts with the world.

Be Authentic

If you constantly try to be someone you're not, you will end up exhausted, frustrated, and unfulfilled. Yes, it may be scary to put yourself out to the world as the "real you," but that's who the world needs! You were created with a certain set of God-given gifts when you were born. Those gifts, combined with your skills, personality traits, and values, make you uniquely you! You are to be celebrated! So don't let what others think hold you back.

Also, by being your authentic self, you give others the permission to do the same. When you are not afraid to be vulnerable, imperfect, and real, others will feel a sense of warmth, compassion, and grace that allows them to relax and be themselves, too. Authentic speakers develop an immediate rapport with their audiences, keeping them engaged throughout their presentation. Those who come across as being perfect and "canned" seem disconnected, and even the best content can be lost with a dry delivery.

Don't Compare Yourself to Others

No two speakers are alike! Everyone starts as a beginner and has a different pathway to their current position. Comparing yourself to someone with more training or years of experience will only set you up for disappointment.

A colleague recently had her first "big time" speaking engagement as one of three keynote speakers for a conference of over a thousand people. She left for the event with confidence, prepared to give a speech that had gotten rave reviews locally. When she arrived, she realized that she was scheduled in between two highly experienced speakers on the agenda, which caused her initial spark of self-doubt. After hearing the first speaker who had a very different delivery style, she immediately went into comparison mode, and decided "on the fly" to try to copy him, rather than staying true to herself. Instead of delivering a speech that was authentic and valuable for her audience, she became distracted and faltered, feeling like a failure afterwards, and it took her days to recover, physically and emotionally.

Instead of comparing your success to another's, compare yourself to *you*. Where were you five years ago? What have you accomplished? How have you grown personally and professionally? What positive changes have you made in your life? You are always becoming a newer version of yourself, so just strive to be the best you, instead of trying to be someone you're not meant to be.

Set Realistic Expectations

Set your expectations on human standards, not super-human. Most likely, you won't be a Zig Ziglar-level speaker in the early days of your speaking career, so set your expectations high enough to stretch you, but not so high that you set yourself up for failure. Becoming a phenomenal speaker takes practice and persistence, and that takes time. Even Oprah Winfrey was told she was "unfit for TV," and she was fired from her job as a television reporter early in her career!

Also, acknowledge that every speech will not be a "home run." It may be your delivery style, the audience, your topic, or the temperature of the room, but there will be times when you don't get all "5s" in your feedback. One speech will not define your entire career, so placing too much importance on each one is not a realistic expectation. Do your best, and then detach yourself from the outcome. Learn from each experience, both the good and the bad points, and keep swinging! Don't leave the game after one strike-out. The world needs you!

> ⇉ *Brilliant Quick Tip* ⇇
>
> *Embrace "Perfect is the enemy of great," and strive for excellence, not perfection. It is much easier than trying to be someone you're not, and it will increase your confidence, enthusiasm, and "likeability."*

Pitfall #2: *Procrastination*

It's easy to put things off, saying that you will get to them later. But eventually later becomes never, and the thought of re-engaging with the task is overwhelming. You accept staying stuck in neutral instead of moving ahead, and prevent yourself from achieving your full potential because it is easier that way. As Michael Dell said, *"There is no guarantee of success, but not doing anything is certainly going to make you fail."*

Don't Allow Perfectionism to Fuel Procrastination

Putting off that first big speech—or speaking professionally at all—is often fueled by perfectionism. When you are worried about delivering a presentation just like the "masters," you become so overwhelmed that you don't even begin. But every speaker has a starting place, and they all started small. Remember the principles of authenticity, comparisons, and expectations that I shared earlier, and when they are feeding your procrastination, take positive action!

Conquer Your Fear

Is fear holding you back from pursuing a speaking career? For too many people, the fear of failure holds them captive in their comfort zones instead of leaping forward with great expectations about the future.

Failure is a natural part of change—if you aren't failing, you aren't growing! Lucille Ball was known as a failed actress and the "Queen of B-List Movies" before landing her role in "I Love Lucy." Sidney Poitier was told to *"Stop wasting people's time and to go out and become a dishwasher"* after his first audition. Michael Jordan missed more than 9,000 shots in his career, and when entrusted to make the game-winning shot, caused his team to lose twenty-six times.

If a fear of failure is feeding your procrastination and stopping you from pursuing your dreams, ask yourself these questions:

> *If I fail, what's the worst that can happen?*

> *How long will it take to recover?*

> *Will it really matter a year from now?*

Then, visualize the very best outcome if you conquer your fear, claim that as your new reality, and start moving!

Take Small Steps Forward

Often, visualizing the task at hand seems daunting and you have no idea where to even begin. Whether it is writing a presentation, marketing yourself as a speaker, or getting on stage that first time, following these steps will make you proactive.

Break a task down into small steps, then put them on a timeline. Trying to accomplish too much at once is daunting and self-defeating.

Start with the hardest task, not the easiest. Do you need to stand in front of a mirror and practice that speech? Do it first, before you check your email. Is it time to "cold call" some prospective clients? Put that high on your daily schedule, before having lunch. Conquering the giants early will feed your energy and enthusiasm for the rest of the day.

Consider how you will feel next week or next month if you don't start today. How much time will you have wasted? And how hard will it be to get caught up?

⋛ *Brilliant Quick Tip* ⋚

When you find yourself procrastinating, make a list of small steps you can take to accomplish a big task. Set a timer for thirty minutes, and work diligently on the first one with no distractions. When thirty minutes are up, celebrate the progress you have made! You might even want to go for another thirty!

Pitfall #3: *Lack of Preparation*

There is simply no substitute for being well-prepared for a presentation. You can have an impressive title, beautifully polished appearance, and a well-written description of your content, but fumbling through your speech shows a lack of respect for your audience, and a lack of commitment to your status as a professional speaker.

I attended a major conference for over 5,000 women from all walks of life who were encouraged to dream big, explore new possibilities, and take positive action to become more successful and fulfilled. Top-notch speakers headlined with messages meant to inspire, challenge, and motivate attendees. While some of the sessions were certainly informative and uplifting, what I remember most were the speakers who fell flat due to lack of preparation.

First, there was a best-selling author who immediately revealed that she had no idea that she was supposed to speak for thirty minutes, and was totally unprepared. To fill her time, she read a chapter from her book causing many people to walk out during her "reading." Then, a highly-respected leader in the financial world stood on the stage with her iPad, scrolling through her presentation as she spoke. Lastly, there was a male speaker who included stories about playing golf to embellish his speech, instead of customizing it for a room filled with women.

The speaker who captivated the entire audience was a Nobel Peace Prize recipient, who spoke from the heart, connected with the crowd, told stories without notes and did not let her broken English stop her from delivering a powerful speech that changed lives that day. She was authentic, passionate and prepared for her audience, fostering mutual respect and immense adoration.

Prepare Well

Research both your topic and your client, customize your presentation for each audience, and don't assume that every speech will fit every group. Write, re-write, and develop an easy-to-remember outline so you will not have to rely on extensive notes. Well-known motivational speaker Brian Tracy says he spends hundreds of hours preparing for every speech, believing that *"Preparation is ninety percent of your success in public speaking."*

Practice

Read your speech out loud, practice in front of a mirror, and video record it so you can review your content and delivery. Be sure your words are easy to pronounce, your eyes are focused on your audience, and your points are clear and effective. Keep track of the time to ensure that you don't exceed your allotment.

Be Primed for Anything that Could Go Wrong

Visualize your presentation, and think about every detail that could fall apart along the way. Do you have a copy of your bio for the host? Do you have a backup plan for your visuals? What would happen to your planned activity if the room had an unexpected layout? Create a complete checklist of every item you need to take along, and every step you need to cover to become comfortable with the room once you arrive. Most importantly, don't let a small calamity ruin your day! If you are well-prepared, little missteps will not even be noticed.

⋛ *Brilliant Quick Tip* ⋚

Send event organizers a questionnaire to gather critical information such as the event theme, attendee demographics, expectations of the speaker, and topics to avoid. Talk to key players to become familiar with the company's culture. The more you know about your audience, the more engaged they will be.

Pitfall #4: *Prima Donna Mentality*

Have you ever been to an event where the speaker mysteriously appeared on stage at just the exact moment of her speech, then disappeared completely as soon as she finished? A professional speaker with a big ego and a large entourage of "handlers" often comes across as stiff and unapproachable. Authentic speakers are magnetic, drawing people to them before they ever step on stage.

Arrive Early

Allow plenty of time to get comfortable with the lighting and the sound, personally doing all the checks. Make sure your visuals can be seen and you can be heard from the back of the room. Taking charge of your own setup shows authority, respect for your host, and professional polish.

Be Genuinely Interested in Meeting the Attendees

Have your preparations complete when the crowd begins arriving, so you can be at ease during any networking time prior to the program. Mingling with the crowd in advance of your presentation builds relationships, establishes trust, and yields interesting tidbits of information that can be woven into your speech from having casual conversations.

Don't Rush Off

Be available after your speech to build strong connections and allow attendees to ask questions and soak in more of your expertise. Sign your books, pose for photos, and exchange contact information with potential clients. Leaving a positive last-impression will increase your chance of a return invitation, as well as a recommendation filled with praise.

⋛ *Brilliant Quick Tip* ⋚

If you are uncomfortable starting conversations, say something like "Tell me about yourself! You will hear enough about me during my presentation."

You have an important message to share with the world! Claim your power over perfectionism, procrastination, lack of preparation, and a prima donna mentality, and you will become a phenomenal speaker soon!

About Susan Tolles

Susan Tolles is the Founder of The Flourishing Life™, a Market Director with the Mentoring Women's Network®, and a Certified Life Purpose Coach® whose clients surround the globe. Her expert guidance leads women to celebrate their unique value, follow their life's calling, and live authentically from the inside out. Susan is a passionate advocate for busy professionals, equipping and motivating them to envision more and reach higher, building a career they love without sacrificing their personal wellbeing. Through Susan's dynamic coaching programs, workshops, and keynote speeches, she teaches them to live, lead, and succeed with purpose for a more meaningful, focused life.

Learn more about Susan Tolles at:
TheFlourishingLife.com

16

⹃Brilliant Advice⹁
from Gabrielle Smith

Speak Easy

When I was first approached to participate in this wonderful work, I immediately agreed. The immediacy of my response leaped from the teacher in me: the part of me that believes knowledge is like currency—it's meant to flow. What an opportunity to share with others the ease of speaking and bringing them to the "other side." When I learned that the work would be include Brilliant Speakers in the title, the speaker in me responded, *"Oh no! What have I gotten myself into?"* (That's the cleaned up version.) From that moment to this one the two have come to a truce, thus my title "Speak Easy," or shall I say, "Speak Easily"?

The reality of speaking is that it *is* easy. Overcoming what makes you believe otherwise is not. In my experience, speaking is about mastering your life's message and liberating others to do the same. Had someone even hinted to me twenty years ago that I would one day be a speaker, I would have rolled on the ground in hysterical laughter. To be among brilliant speakers I would have looked behind curtains and into closets for the hidden *Candid Camera*. So here I am. Please know and understand that this is not a discourse in shattered esteem and feeble self-confidence, but rather my awe-filled response of discovering *who* I am as I have searched to find *what* I am. It is to this end that I know for sure that being a speaker is less than you probably think and more than you can imagine.

⋛ *Brilliant Quick Tip* ⋚

Speaking is easy if you can overcome what makes you believe otherwise.

Re-*Imag*-ine

It is said that a picture is worth a thousand words; in my experience I have come to find that a word holds a thousand images. Over the past couple of decades I have started off most of my workshops and seminars with a little exercise in cognitive behavior. I like to do this in an effort to break all of the would-be distractions that are simply a part of our human nature and human experiences. I ask the participants to number a sheet of paper from one to four. I then give them the following rules:

> *"I will give you three words. I will say, 'number one' and the word; 'number two' and the word; and 'number three' and the word. I will not repeat a word nor will I define or explain a word. When I say the word, write down the first thing that comes to your mind-* **do not censor!** *I will then repeat the number and the corresponding word and I want you to shout out whatever you have written until we get to the end."*

Some people have referred to this exercise as an icebreaker; I refer to it as an alarm clock that wakes us up from the past and heightens our consciousness to the present moment.

My usual three words are *"cup," "pen,"* and *"joint."* As you might imagine, the answers go from predictable to downright funny. The first word, cup, usually renders such responses as beverages and other accoutrements such as saucers and straws. The same occurs with pen: writing instruments, paper, ink, etc. The third word, joint, brings a range of responses from body parts to herbs used to treat glaucoma (smile).

During a session with a group of high-school students, I heard a most unusual response to the second word, pen. When I recited the word I heard a vehement, *"Don't want to go!"* Shocked and bewildered, I had to stop for an explanation. The young man repeated, *"Don't want to go, ma'am!"* We all looked around at each other as if someone had the missing clue to this riddle.

The young man repeated once again, *"I don't want to go to the penitentiary!"* We continued our gaze and like clockwork burst into laughter. I later learned that the group had been participating in a series called *Scared Straight* where they were able to interface with their peers who chose crime over education. It went without saying that the program was effective for him. The point of this exercise is to not only unlock their thoughts and way of thinking, but to also reveal the process and references to them.

Now, if you remember previously, I asked the participants to number the sheets up to four. After I debrief them from the first three words I allow them to regain their composure because I never cease to be amazed by what this exercise does. As I move on to the fourth, I know that without fail the phrase will ascend us to exactly where I want us to land. My instructions are as follows: *"The next phrase I will recite is to* *you and you alone. Pretend that no one else is in the room. Whatever image, word, or feeling comes to your mind, write it down. Number four, **I love you**."*

If I were to write down the varying responses I have gotten over the years, I could compile an entire book. I have been a recipient of everything from *"I love you too,"* to the most interesting combination and compounding of profanity, to people storming out of the room. This phrase always proves to be the breaking point, or rather the tipping point—the most common response centering something about me not *knowing* them and how could I love them. I usually rebut with two questions, 1) *"Have you ever disliked someone or been the person someone else disliked, and neither of you knew each other?"* One hundred percent of the time the answer is, *"Yes."* 2) *"Did you tell them or yourself that this dislike could not be possible or authentic, since you did not know each other?"* The answer is always 100 percent, "No." The latter answer is usually accompanied by some sign of an epiphany.

The point here is that we are mostly living with thoughts, beliefs, and images of something that never was and/or is not present or accurate. If you can translate this process to your thinking of being a speaker, you have just crossed over to what it means to be a **brilliant speaker**; congratulations! Being a speaker is more than likely not what you believe or imagine.

Though there are basic semantics that are required, I would gamble that those are not the things you find yourself challenged by. I can say this because after years, I still shrug a bit when I hear someone refer to me as such; not because I don't know it or own it, but because I know some of the images that others see when they hear the title. (Remember, cup, pen, joint, and *"I love you"*?) And I don't want to mold myself into those images.

Whether you are a speaker and want to speak more, or you are a speaker and want to expand your platform, or if you want to become a speaker, you must reconcile your image of being a speaker to one that supports who you are and what you can do. Do not "Imag-ine" yourself *out of* it, imagine yourself *into* it; get the appropriate image necessary to move forward by expanding your definition and belief about what it means to be a speaker. If there are deficiencies you think you have, hone them through practice, not theory. Practice makes better. You can do it!

⋛ *Brilliant Quick Tip* ⋚

*Do not "Imag-ine" yourself out of it,
imagine yourself into it.*

Verb Versus Noun

Earlier I spoke of my having to overcome my images of what I imagined others thought being a speaker would mean. Let me now share how I overcame this struggle. I am part of a geographical society, a sisterhood, that functions under the acronym GRITS: Girls Raised In The South. As you can imagine, I was born into this sisterhood so I didn't have to submit an application or go before a board for initiation or approval—I am a legacy. With all of the things that might be characteristic (or even stereotypical) of being southern, I not only have the twang but I grew up with a big voice; to this day I still cannot whisper because my voice tone will carry the message. Because of this, anytime I would talk, people would turn around to see who was saying what. Often, they did not think I was a kid because my voice was so full and rich. Though most of the adults thought it was pretty fascinating, kids did not and I was always challenged in some way.

My beloved parents made sure our family traveled every year. Whether it was the beaches of Florida, the wonders of Disney World, or family reunions, we would pile into the family car with freshly fried chicken, ham and cheese sandwiches, snacks, and a cooler of soda and juice in tow. As we travelled, I became immune to people coming up to me and requesting that I *"Talk!"* or *"Say something!"* So, not only was this voice not working for me at home, it was not working abroad. By the time I reached high school and college, I had grown into my voice—or maybe I had surrendered to what it was and what it was not. Funny thing, it was almost with clockwork precision that when I embraced and loved my voice, so did others. Platforms began to appear, where I was unanimously chosen to MC programs and ceremonies, as well as make appearances at conferences and workshops. The most lasting lesson I gained from this seemingly long journey is that being a speaker is first *who you are* and then *what you do*.

Most people who know my husband know that he is a quiet storm. He is an impeccable listener, so when he speaks he usually has something pretty profound to say. The other thing that people know about my beloved is that he loves music! Some people quote philosophers; he quotes great song writers and lyricists. In his hay day he was a fierce DJ and at the top of the list for events. If you were to walk into his man-cave you would be met by four to six tower speakers. Now, when I say *speakers*, I don't mean those little discreet cubes that you spread around the room for surround sound. These things are the size of elementary-school kids! Though I have attempted to woo him with something a little less scary, he is committed to them and to the technology that cannot be paralleled.

Since I believe there is a lesson in everything, I sought to find my lesson in these speakers, and here is what I learned . . . we are one in the same! The purpose of any great or brilliant (or even life-sized) speaker is not to *be* but rather to *do*. As a speaker, my purpose is to give voice and to amplify sound—to amplify sound to those who may not otherwise have access to hear; to those whose senses have been dulled by circumstances or lack thereof; to amplify faint whispers to parts of the human spirit that are experiencing deafness from the accumulation of losses; to amplify sounds that will hush the clamor of fear, distrust, and degradation.

As speakers, we are the platform, and our voices are our instruments. The brilliancy of being a speaker is that we each get to do this in our own unique way. The sooner you realize this, the sooner you will rest in the ease of speaking. The sooner you can rest in this ease, the sooner you will lose the need to compare yourself to any other speaker. To admire is one thing, to compare is to destroy.

⋛ *Brilliant Quick Tip* ⋚

The purpose of any brilliant speaker is not to be but rather to do. Give a voice to something meaningful; amplify sound to those who need to hear that sound.

To Be or Not to Be

As I stated earlier, speaking has long been—and continues to be—thought of as something that is mystical, out of reach, and downright scary. I am often asked by others if I think *they* could a speaker. My response centers something to the effect that being a speaker is something you can *not* be, as opposed to something you can be; there is a difference. There are many things most of us can do or be, if you will. But there are few things we can *not* be. I am often asked if I am a makeup artist or if I sell cosmetics, and though I like to use makeup and have an appreciation for the artistry, I went most of the summer without using makeup. I love to bake; it is most therapeutic for me, but I have not baked anything since Mother's day and nothing before that except for the Christmas holidays. There were periods of my life where I baked every weekend and went through my neighborhood passing out cakes and cookies, but it was years ago (by the way, my neighbors have an all-points bulletin out for that girl!). There are many things I can do because I have a love for it or some level of skilled training. What I've learned over the years is that which defines us are the things we cannot *not* do.

I have come to know myself as a problem solver, a teacher, a counselor, a motivator (or maybe even an agitator—I love to challenge the status quo), and a healer; I have done this in some form or fashion all of my life. Though I have done this at many levels, speaking is the medium that allows my voice to be carried and to amplify solutions, lessons, counsel, motivation, and healing to others. Whether it is 1 or 100,001, it's all the same to me; whether it's the hair salon or the arena, this is who I am when I am asleep and when I am awake.

Your Turn

I personally believe that there is a speaker in everyone. My mantra of many years remains "*Teaching is the rent that you pay to live on earth*" (Marian Wright Edelman). Whether you are exploring or expanding the idea of being a speaker, or simply exploring the possibility of all that you are, please take some time to answer the following questions. Give yourself ninety days to explore and meditate on the possible answers; you will be amazed.

1. What things are you most passionate about?

2. Why are you passionate about them?

3. How far does this passion span across your life (employ relatives and friends to help you with this one)?

4. What has your response been to this passion(s)?

5. What role do you see yourself playing in the future?

6. Is there "sound" that needs to be amplified?

7. What is your image of speaking? Of *yourself* speaking?

8. Can you *Speak Easy*?

About Gabrielle Smith

Helping others realize their professional potentials, and developing leadership abilities, has long time colored Gabrielle "Gabbe" Smith's life and career. Her training in psychology, together with her industry/organization specialization, has allowed her to make significant inroads into the local community of the Dallas-Fort Worth area, as well as on a national level, with motivational speaking and training through her consulting firm, Visionaires.

Known as the "trainer's trainer" and the "coach's coach," Gabrielle works with organizations and individuals who are experiencing blocks and seemingly insurmountable hurdles, to help them achieve their goals and facilitate change.

Learn more about Gabrielle Smith at: VisionairesConsultingGroup.com

17

≷Brilliant Advice≷
from Elisha

3 Powerful Ways to Authenticity

Have you ever thought that if you truly acted as yourself while speaking, you would be criticized or judged by others?

Even though I am only twelve years old, as I write this, I have spoken in front of many audiences of children, and even men and women, about the subjects of self-esteem and being confident in who you are. I love speaking onstage and sharing who I am with others, and my speaking ability has become one of my most memorable traits, but it wasn't always that way. I used to have a big fear that if I was myself onstage, I would be considered unprofessional or I would be ignored. Thankfully, my mom helped me overcome that fear and showed me that when we are ourselves and act freely onstage and offstage, we can build trust with our audience and truly connect with them.

You too can be yourself onstage and become memorable to others, not just through what you say, but through who you are! I want to share with you three ways I believe you can be authentic and be your true self.

1. Tell Your Story!

> *"Owning our story can be hard but not nearly as difficult as spending our lives running from it.*

Embracing our vulnerabilities is risky but not nearly as dangerous as giving up on love and belonging and joy—the experiences that make us the most vulnerable. Only when we are brave enough to explore the darkness will we discover the infinite power of our light." -Brené Brown

I know we all have embarrassing stories and can tell of times when we have failed and made mistakes, but isn't it easier to share them instead of wasting our life running away?

> ⦆ *Brilliant Quick Tip* ⦅
>
> *It is easier to share an embarrassing story than it is to waste time running from it, especially when it can help someone else.*

As speakers, we must be **FOV** with our audiences! Here's what that means:

F: *Frank*

We must be direct with our audience, and share our opinions. We must not hold anything back, but also do it with kindness and gentleness. Franz Kafka says this beautifully, "*Don't bend; don't water it down; don't try to make it logical; don't edit your own soul according to the fashion. Rather, follow your most intense obsessions mercilessly."*

O: *Open*

We must speak the whole truth about everything. I used to exaggerate and stretch the truth, and I have lost trust from family members and friends. Now I make sure I say exactly how everything happened, with every relevant detail. Our stories may be sad, terrifying, or even traumatizing, but we must remember that we are all human and we can all relate to each other and connect with each other.

I love what Charles Dickens says about this matter: *"To conceal anything from those to whom I am attached, is not in my nature. I can never close my lips where I have opened my heart."*

V: *Vulnerable*

In my experiences with public speaking, this part has always been difficult for me. I find it increasingly difficult to cry in front of an audience. When we express our feelings there is a complete change in the audience. They pay more attention to your tone, facial expressions and hand movements.

There was a particular occasion in which my sister, mom, and I were in the car driving to a speaking engagement. Elyssa suggested that she should share a story about our father—who left us when we were one and two years old—and how we both felt about it in the past. I knew I would be very uncomfortable sharing that story. My mom said that either Elyssa could say "we" and I could simply nod my head, or she could share it on her own and say "I" statements. My mom then told me that we can heal through sharing painful stories, but that it was okay to choose not to share until I felt ready. When it was time for our presentation, I felt that the ladies there needed that message and I actually shared the story with tears in my eyes. Later on, my mom commented that it was very brave to share the story on my own. After that, not only I felt relief to finally get that off my chest, but professionally, it allows me to tell the same story to other people who need that message—without the fear! When you show your vulnerabilities, you show your ultimate strength.

2. Remember that You Bring Value!

We have all felt that maybe what we have to say or offer is not important. But, just imagine how boring and dull life would be if we were all the same! God created us all to complement and learn from each other. You have knowledge, wisdom, and expertise that others do not have. You are unique, so make sure you share and spread that uniqueness. We all bring a different flavor to the world. I love the saying *"It takes all kinds of people to make the world go round."* Remember that you are valuable and your audience will see the value you bring to others. Never underestimate who you are, because you are capable of great things. I always feel really happy when I know my message has influenced and helped others. It is amazing to know that everything you say and write can be for the benefit of others.

> ⋛ *Brilliant Quick Tip* ⋚
>
> *You are capable of great things; never underestimate who you are.*

3. Ignore the Critics!

When you are yourself in front of an audience, they respect you and you feel good about yourself; you feel like you don't have to pretend and you don't have to be like someone else. After speaking in front of a small audience of women, one of them confessed that she had previously thought *"What can an eleven-year-old teach me?"* And then she said that my message applied to her and she was grateful for it, and she took notes!

However, there will be more vocal haters and judges who will try to make you feel bad about yourself. If you listen to those people, you won't be yourself in front of others and you won't be able to do your absolute best. The saying *"Misery loves company"* is very true. People who are upset or angry want you to join the pity party. Ignore the invitation to "Lonely Island." Be yourself and be proud about who you are.

≥ *Brilliant Quick Tip* ≤

People who are upset or angry want you to join the pity party. Ignore them. Be yourself and be proud of who you are.

Also, never compare yourself to other speakers. When you compare, you diminish yourself, which makes you less confident on the stage. Comparing yourself to others can lead to trying to be like someone else, which can lead to self-destructing habits.

I am the youngest member of the Women Speakers Association (WSA), and being part of their team, I designed an infographic for them and I posted the pictures on the WSA group Pinterest board. I later noticed a comment on one of them from a man saying that the color was not good enough and I did a bad job with the picture, and he even offered his services to the group. I felt outraged and upset, and thankfully, my mom reminded me that no one's opinion matters but mine, and she has always taught me to "consider the source." We then proceeded to look at his Pinterest board and found out that his pictures were a bit embarrassing! So, in the end, I felt sorry for his insecurity, and I continued to feel proud about the good job I did. This is the moral: believe in yourself and know you are special, and you will do a better job speaking.

Remember that being authentic is a great tool for your speaking business. It means:

1. Being sincere with yourself and others, not pretending

2. Fearlessly knowing and being who you are

3. Paying attention to your opinion, not others'

When you follow these guidelines, you will be successful, confident, and, most importantly, HAPPY!

About Elisha

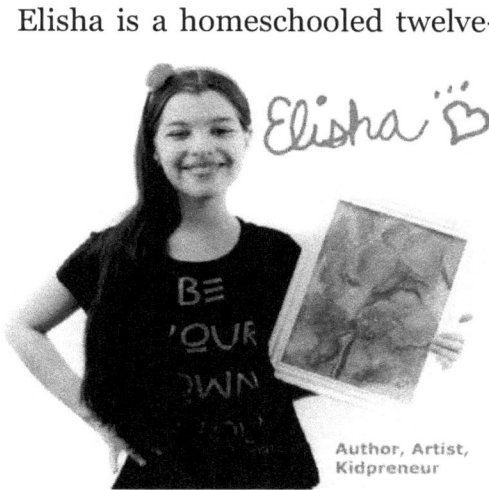

Elisha is a homeschooled twelve-year-old, and a passionate author, artist, kidpreneur, and speaker. She loves to write, read, spell, draw, paint, and play the piano and guitar. She is proud to be a Certified Guerrilla Marketing Practitioner, trained by Jay Conrad Levinson himself.

If Elisha had only three words to describe herself they would be creative, generous, and humorous. Elisha lives in Dallas, TX with her family, and she loves spending time with them. She wrote *I Love ME*! at age ten, because she is passionate about helping other kids become bully-proof, love themselves, and be the best they can be.

Learn more about Elisha at:
WhollyART.com

18

≷Brilliant Advice≷
from Elyssa

Get Out Of Your Own Way and Shine

"According to most studies, people's number one fear is public speaking. Number two is death. Death is number two. Does that sound right? This means to the average person, if you go to a funeral, you're better off in the casket than doing the eulogy." -Jerry Seinfeld

Do you ever get a little nervous or queasy when you're in the spotlight? Fear is your BIG obstacle to making your mark in this world.

You may be wondering, *"Can we possibly get rid our fear permanently?"* The answer is no. Fear is naturally a part of us, but we can prevent it from controlling everything we do and don't do.

As Nelson Mandela said, *"I learned that courage was not the absence of fear, but the triumph over it. The brave man is not he who does not feel afraid, but he who conquers that fear."*

Fear causes negative self-talk: that little voice in your head that is always discouraging you. It is always making up excuses on why you can't do something. Did you know seventy-seven percent of our self-talk is negative?

In school, we all learned about facts and opinions, right? Facts have little pieces of information that support them, and to me, negative self-talk, a.k.a. your inner bully, supports your fear just like that. Our inner bully makes up excuses, blames self and others, and constantly taunts us.

Some of the inner bully's favorite excuses are:

1. *"I'm too . . . (big/small)"*

2. *"I'm not (old/young) enough to do that."*

3. *"I'm not as (cool) as everyone else."*

4. *"I'm so horrible at this."*

5. *"I'll NEVER be like that."*

And the list goes on . . .

There are three main reasons we bully ourselves:

1. Constant criticism

Sometimes when people criticize us, it becomes a natural part of our thinking system. Repeated criticism = your thinking system.

2. Jumping to negative conclusions

When we jump to negative conclusions, we become so discouraged we might not even do that thing. Someone once said, *"You miss 100 percent of the shots you don't take."*

3. Taking things personally

Bad things happen to all of us. When we take things personally, we constantly wonder, *"What did I do to deserve this?"* Tony Robbins says our brain is a super computer, so it always finds an answer. It might say *"Maybe, it's just that, they don't like YOU."*

⋧ *Brilliant Quick Tip* ⋦

Don't jump to negative conclusions, or you won't even try a thing. If you never try, you can never "make the shot."

As I write this, my sister and I are eleven and twelve years old, respectively, and we created a company called WhollyART so we can teach positive values through art. We are also authors, and co-wrote a book that helps kids improve their self-esteem, called *I Love ME!* Because of this, we are invited to speak at many events.

Not too long ago, I was selected to speak before a group of teens, who were older than us. I was very nervous and afraid about doing this. But, I knew in my heart this group needed my message.

My mom said: *"Just speak from your heart."* My inner bully kept on making excuses and taunts, but I pushed them away with all my might.

Finally, the time had come. I went up there, did a great job teaching and inspiring the audience, and conquered my fear.

A letter from Abraham Lincoln to a Republican political committee that previously asked him to give a speech is a perfect example of how everyone feels some level of fear, maybe not always, but sometimes because of certain emotions or circumstances. Here's the full note from Abe Lincoln dated March 6, 1860:

> Yours of the 2nd was received late last evening. I cannot speak in New Jersey this time. I have over staid my time—have heard something about sickness in my family—and really am nervous and unfit to fill my engagement already made here in Connecticut. Will you please excuse me?
>
> Yours Respectfully,
>
> A. Lincoln

It sounds to me like a manner of negative self-talk, and discounting self. Does it sound like that to you, as well? This is one of the greatest men in history, yet he had fears, too. So, we are not alone in our pursuit of not letting our fear control us and our actions.

Have you ever heard the saying *"Get out of your own way"*? That's what you must do to stop your inner bully from controlling your life. But how?

I will teach you a five-step system to help you prevent your fears and your inner bully from interfering with you achieving your goals and dreams.

Step 1: *Focus On Your Audience*

Instead of focusing on what you may be doing wrong, focus on what you can do to help the audience. This helps us forget about worries, such as, "*I probably look like a fool right now. I can't do this!*"

If you're not thinking about your audience (specifically, your target market), you don't impact anybody. And without impact, there is ultimately, no income; and with no income, we can't make a difference anymore!

Step 2: *Talk Back*

As little children, we are taught to *never talk back*. But not now! Whenever, wherever, whatever it is, if you hear your inner bully beating you up, talk back! That'll give it something to think about!

Something I like to say is, "*You think I can't? Think again, my friend, think again.*" It doesn't matter how you do it, or even how you say it, face your fear!

C. JoyBell C. said, "*Don't be afraid of your fears. They're not there to scare you. They're there to let you know that something is worth it.*"

> ### ≷ *Brilliant Quick Tip* ≷
>
> *Whenever, wherever, whatever it is*
> *your inner bully says, talk back!*

Step 3: *Forget About It!*

Forget your fear! Someone out there might be in a situation *right now* and the only person who can make a change, is you. *You!* Not Freddy, or Sally, or even Mike, it's you and your message that can make a difference. If you don't make your mark, no one else will do it for you. Your message and mission is BIGGER than whatever fear you have.

Ambrose Redmoon said something that illustrates this very well: *"Courage is not the absence of fear, but rather the judgment that something else is more important than fear."*

Step 4: *Prove it WRONG!*

When you daily tune in to the lies of the inner bully, the lies turn into reality, and we officially prove it right.

So, prove that you aren't a teensy bit as horrible as that bully wants you to believe you are.

If you have been procrastinating because of negative self-talk or your fears, prove your bully wrong by taking action!

≥ *Brilliant Quick Tip* ≤

Prove your inner bully wrong
by taking action.

Step 5: *Make it a Tool*

You can use fear as a tool to be an even better speaker. Fear can turn into your motivation to get up there and speak: fear of wasting your time on Earth without making an impact, fear of not making a difference—that kind of fear—will make you get up every morning ready to praise the Lord for a new day to face your fear.

I used to have the fear that since I am young and people comment that I'm cute, they won't take me seriously. In fact, I thought that when they would oooooooh and awwwwwww, it meant they weren't paying attention. That was my inner bully. It tells us lies, but they are only true if we believe them. I listened to my mom instead, and I chose to believe the very same things I doubted were actually an advantage to me, and drew attention to what I was saying—my message of inspiration to others—and this helped me focus better.

My call-to-action and my challenge for you is to face your fear . . . *today*!

Marie Curie said, "*Nothing in life is to be feared, it is only to be understood. Now is the time to understand more, so that we may fear less.*"

Be an example!

About Elyssa

Elyssa is eleven years old. She enjoys being an entrepreneur, speaker, author, artist, and coach. She is homeschooled, and her greatest coach and mentor is her mom, Elayna Fernández.

Elyssa plays the guitar and piano, and she loves to play with her sister, draw, read, write stories, dance ballet, play tennis, and bike. She's fascinated with nature, especially animals, and to avoid hurting them, she became vegan.

Author, Artist, Kidpreneur
WhollyART.com

Elyssa teaches children to love themselves and have self-confidence through her books, blog posts, and artistic expressions. Elyssa would be thrilled to get to know you.

Learn more about Elyssa at:
WhollyArt.com

19

≥Brilliant Advice≤
from Kimberly Pitts

Warning Signs Your Speaking Business is Dying, not Growing

I remember the day I heard her speak. She was so poised, beautiful, and powerful, all in a five-foot, four-inch frame. She was supposed to deliver what typically is a general, "less than enthusiastic" training presentation to a room of 150 employees (who were required to attend). So you can probably guess they were not excited about being there.

So when she opened her mouth to deliver her presentation, she shocked everyone. She immediately had everyone on their feet to do some dance moves to wake up them up; she put on some great music, and after she had everyone laughing and smiling, she launched into one of the most engaging and energetic presentations I have ever heard. What struck me the most is that she took what could be deemed "boring" content and made it lively, engaging, and highly interactive.

This was fifteen years ago and to this day her presentation was still one of the best I've ever heard. After her training that day she asked me if I would help market her as a speaker. She knew I was working on my MBA specializing in marketing, and I was fresh out of college. So I was excited and eager to work on something creative.

I had no idea what helping someone become a marketable speaker would entail and what it would look like to brand her. However, I dug in and learned from some of the best of the best in the industry. I spent eight years working with professional speakers, people aspiring to become professional speakers, speakers on the way up, and all the variants in between. I handled their marketing, positioned their brand in their industry, and handled everything for them. The road was not easy and I learned so much about what meeting planners look for, what they are drawn, to and how to best reach out to them.

I have seen this industry from a unique perspective that many have not experienced. It takes more than a beautiful glossy one sheet, a list of great sounding presentations, and trying to be seen in every place possible. Truly launching your speaking career is rooted in how you choose to enter the market and how you position yourself in front of the meeting planners who can place you in front of their audience.

While I no longer work with speakers in that capacity—since I started UImpact a few years ago—I want to impart to you what I've learned and still witness today that can help you position yourself as an in-demand speaker. Let's look at potential warning signs that your speaking business is dying and/or not growing.

Have you ever been in a position where you try to warn someone that they are headed in the wrong direction, but they refuse to listen to you? Better yet, they refuse to see the warning signs? It is hard to witness when those blaring warning signs are ignored.

However, I want to list below potential reasons why things may not be growing as you hoped they would. This list is great for you even if your speaker business is growing. Why? It allows you to see trouble before it comes.

Let's Make a Deal

You're constantly being asked to discount your prices and you feel you have no option but to do so. You are stuck in the rut of *"My fee is $2500, however I am open to accepting whatever your budget is."* The problem with this model is that you can easily develop a reputation that you're available to speak at a bargain. Not to sound all "woo-woo," but this does go back to the *Law of Attraction*; you attract what you put there.

Suggestion to Avoid This

Meeting/conference planners love to price shop, however, when you really communicate your value and address all their objections (before they state them) in your marketing copy, you reduce attracting price shoppers. They will pay for the value that you present. This is more than the speaker sheet and a beautiful website. Meeting/conference planners are researching speakers online to see who they are outside of the professional website.

They are looking to see if what you present as your value lines up with who they see when they research you. So ensure that all the entry points into your business communicate a clear and consistent message about who you are as a speaker.

⋛ *Brilliant Quick Tip* ⋞

Event planners pay for the value you present. Communicate value and address all objections in your marketing copy.

Trying to Catch Their Attention

You keep changing who you want to be known as to fit your latest marketing campaign and/or advertisement. One day you are a clarity speaker, next month you are speaking about goal setting, and a few months later you feel you are a leadership expert. You are constantly changing what you want to be known as to fit what you believe is marketable.

Suggestion to Avoid This

While this may sound cliché, you must stay true to yourself. Yes, you do need to ensure that what you want to speak on is marketable. However, avoid speaking on topics you know you are not proficient in for the sake of getting speaking engagements.

No Diversity

You only offer one signature talk and that is it. Yes, you should have a signature talk but if that is all you offer, you will not provide the meeting planner with options. Meeting planners love to book speakers who will keynote and offer a workshop as well. Doing both provides you with an opportunity to allow your audience to get to know you better.

Additionally, offer different ways to engage your audience. This is another form of diversity in your speaking business. If you think back on the best speakers you have heard speak, your mind will recall something they did or said that really created an imprint on you. Are you creating different ways to engage your audience? Are you creating a memorable presentation?

Suggestion to Avoid This

Sometimes, when you experience great results with one talk, you tend to want to stay with just that talk. If you are a keynote speaker, have one to two main keynote speeches and two to three workshop topics. More importantly, ensure that the topics you wish to speak on are in line with the current issues of your audience. The best speakers out there are infusing current trends and data with their established presentations.

⋛ *Brilliant Quick Tip* ⋚

The best speakers infuse current trends and data with their established presentations.

Lack of Genuineness

I believe there is such a strong presence out there of what I call "The Frankenstein Model," where people build their speaking brand using pieces of everything they see and feel will help them launch strongly and become known, versus constructing their brand based on who they are. As much as we talk about being different, there is still a lot of sameness going on. I don't want to see that for you. That is why I wanted to bring this up. It is great to look at those you admire, but then go back and hone and construct what makes you stand out.

Suggestion to Avoid This

The speakers who are the most booked . . . the most known, all stand out because they choose to present their information in their own voice, using methods they connect to. For example, Tony Robbins is known for fire walking, Les Brown for his story about his grandmother, John Maxwell for being a thought leader on leadership, Suze Orman for her strong, yet effective way of delivering financial information.

If you look at each person I mentioned, you will see that each has a distinct way of presenting information. When people think about you, what do they think of? What makes your message distinctive? How are you delivering your message?

The next area I want to dive into is one that is not covered often in this arena. If you look at the speakers you admire and wish to model, you will quickly notice that you are drawn to them for a reason. Maybe they made you laugh, cry, or think. Maybe they made you want to do better, be better, or step out in a new direction. Whatever it is they made you feel, what they created was an emotional connection with you. That emotional connection could be an array of different things, like excitement, intrigue, renewed hope, conviction, a sense of encouragement, and the list goes on.

Once that emotional connection has been established, you stay plugged in to all that they do. The same goes for speaking. Once you established a great emotional connection with your audience they will want to stay connected to you, work with you, buy from you, and learn from you.

Are You Creating This Type of Connection?

Maya Angelou said, *"People won't remember what you said, but they will remember how you made them feel."* This is the core of an influential personal and business brand. To make a true impact and resonate strongly with your target audience, you've got to make an emotional connection. Fifty percent of every buying decision is driven by emotion. Emotions shape the attitudes that drive decisions and behavior.

The most powerful question you can ask yourself as a speaker is, "*How do I want people to FEEL when they hear my presentation?*"

As you are asking yourself that question, I want you to also take the time and ask yourself the following:

⋛ *Do people connect with the information I am sharing?*

⋛ *How am I getting to know my audience as people and not just potential clients?*

⋛ *How is my client care engagement process with the meeting planners I work with?*

⋛ *Brilliant Quick Tip* ⋚

As a speaker, the most powerful question you can ask yourself is, "How do I want people to FEEL when they hear my presentation?"

How Do You Build and Strengthen these Connections? Look Under the Hood

Examine your processes, procedures, and even the messages you send to meeting planners. Where is the focus? Is it on you, or on the audiences you want to attract? Every time you speak, ask yourself, *"If I were in the audience, how would this experience feel for me? Did I enjoy how this speaker engaged me? Did I get any value from listening to them? Did the meeting planner feel working with me was simple and easy?"* Consistently examining your processes helps illuminate areas of strengths and opportunities for growth.

Plug In

Make a point to regularly listen to your market, to the meeting planners, and to what your attendees say. Listen for validation or inconsistencies with your image and presentation. Do you regularly listen and seek to understand how you can grow as a speaker? Listening can be a challenge because it means you have to be open to hearing what your audience and meeting planners like and dislike about your presentation.

Additionally staying on top of what is taking place in your market is equally important. I cannot begin to tell you how many speakers I knew who used presentations that were filled with outdated content.

In a day and age where information is changing rapidly and people have access to so much, you must stay current on what is taking place. This will ensure that your presentations are relevant, and engaging, and it positions you as someone others can trust.

In Closing

My hope and prayer is that you really and truly hold a mirror up to yourself and ask the questions I posed, and be honest about where you are right now. Over the years I have worked with many speakers and I can honesty tell you that the ones who make it are the ones who look into that mirror.

I wrote this because I want each person who decides to buy this book to read all the great content from each author, and grow to become a stronger, more in-demand speaker. Be aware of the warning signs and create that emotional connection with your audience.

About Kimberly Pitts

Kimberly Pitts is a both a branding & marketing strategist and developer, dedicated to helping women entrepreneurs use branding and marketing strategies to position their businesses in the market, attract their target audiences, create influential brands, realize more income, and enjoy freedom in both their businesses and their lives. She does this through her premier training-based mastermind program (Thrive Academy), her Branding VIP Program, the Packaged for Growth Annual Conference, and a myriad of ongoing training programs.

Anything but conventional, Kimberly is here to provide expert coaching and mentoring to better position you and your business for greater influence.

Learn more about Kimberly Pitts at: Uimpact.net

20

⋛Brilliant Advice⋚
from Kathy Kingston

Propel Your Speaking—Publish Your Book:
A Trio of Insider Tips

As a top speaker in the fields of fundraising, auctions, and consulting, I'm thrilled that my first book published by John Wiley and Sons, Inc. entitled *A Higher Bid: How to Transform Special Event Fundraising with Strategic Benefit Auctions*, will be released mid 2015.

Writing a commercially published book can help you grow your speaking business and establish yourself as an expert in your profession. In this chapter, I share three of my proven strategies to build your community, create your unique body of work, increase clients, and propel new speaking business—all of which can be attractive to publishers.

First, a True Story

Drenched one day, several years ago in the pouring rain, I was not excited about slogging to my local dry cleaners, just to grab my ball gown, especially when I had to conduct a charity auction gala that night.

I opened the door of the dry cleaners, surprised to find a long line. When it was my turn, I noticed a cardboard sign taped prominently on the front of the cash register, forcefully handwritten with bold, blue ink. Signed proudly by the dry cleaner owner and her husband it read, *"I refuse to participate in this recession."*

As I paid for my ball gown, I remarked, *"Kim, I really like your sign. What do you mean, you refuse to participate in the recession?"* She simply smiled and said, *"Oh yes!*

We are making our own economy. Thank you, Kathy, so much for your business. I'm glad you're happy with your beautiful dress. It really means so much that you come to us. See you next time."

I loved their fantastic attitude, so I zoomed back to my office and immediately made my own sign, *"I create my own economy."* I've taken that mantra to heart, and the last several years, my speaking and benefit auction business are the strongest yet—in nearly three decades in business—both financially and in terms of personal satisfaction in working with clients.

Create Your Own Economy

To create my own new economy, I invested in professional development workshops and top coaches to improve my speaking, auctioneering, consulting, and entrepreneurial skills. Mentors empowered me to go beyond my limiting mindset of one-time events where I could only impact the audience in that room.

So, I transformed my speaking and auction business model by applying this powerful lesson: provide greater value by sharing my expertise through writing, teaching, and giving back. These strategies have turbo-charged my business and positively improved my quality of life. Most importantly, my work has significantly transformed the lives of people, animals, organizations, and communities, and advanced my industry.

I was so excited about the success of my new expanded business model. (My business more than doubled that year.) I felt compelled to write a book. In *A Higher Bid* I wanted to help others create their own new economy by showcasing this same paradigm shift for the world of fundraising and donor development. Strategic benefit auctions are a powerful catalyst for donors to make a long-term impact. When designed and conducted strategically, benefit auctions are one of the most powerful ways to raise billions more charitable dollars annually.

Sadly, many organizers mistakenly downplay events and benefit auctions as a one-time party, and so leave untold thousands upon thousands of dollars in the room every year. And worse yet, because of this limiting view, many donors are never invited to stay connected. They simply leave and take their energy and dollars to another organization. (This applies to the speaking business too. Create your vibrant community to be a catalyst for cultivating long-term clients.)

And now I'm delighted that so many people will have the chance to read my book and to discover how my dynamic strategies will significantly transform causes that impassion them.

Go Beyond the Platform

If you are interested in writing a book, it's important to know that publishers select authors for myriad reasons, including but not limited to interest in your subject matter, interest in you as an author, and interest in your expertise; but also because you have a large community of followers that will give you the capacity to sell more books.

"It's not about what you get; it's how much you give that makes a difference." That's my core message to charity auction

audiences. (That's how I sold a tangy tangerine for $2,500!) This compelling concept applies to you and your speaking career, too. How much can you give to your audience, to your community, and to people you care about to make a difference?

My trio of business-builder strategies can help you boost your speaking business while strategically designing leverage for you as an author to publish your book.

1. Write: *Spread Your Expertise*

Bring greater value to your audience and position yourself as a thought leader in your niche. Spread your knowledge by writing articles and blog posts about your thinking on current trends, best practices, your tried-and-true unique approaches to challenges, what works, and what flops. Just get out there in print. Create an e-newsletter, blog, comment on other's blogs. Write articles and opinion editorials for other newsletters, magazines, and trade publications, and be sure to post all your materials on your social media outlets such as Facebook, LinkedIn, Twitter, Pinterest, and others. Promote your writing prominently on your website.

Writing is a fantastic way to position yourself as an expert thought leader who takes clients to the next level. The best bonus of writing is that you continue to hone your writing and clarify your thinking while building a portfolio of your work as a basis for your book and other products. These products can be sold from the platform and in the back of the room.

> ⋛ *Brilliant Quick Tip* ⋚
>
> *Writing allows you to build a body of your work as a basis for your book and products.*

Since adopting this core strategy, I've penned countless articles and stories for my blog and monthly complimentary e-newsletter (called BIDhi!); been a guest writer for magazines, newsletters, and social media sites; and built a strong database of loyal followers from Cape Cod to Cape Town.

2. Stand Out: *Conduct Your Own Seminars*

Creating and teaching my own seminars, workshops, webinars, and tele-seminars, are the heart and soul of my marketing strategy as a speaker and auctioneer. Many times I'll get booked for numerous new events by seminar attendees, even before lunch.

Because I offer my own highly interactive, content-rich, live seminars, tele-seminars, and custom workshops, I'm distinctly different than my competition.

Decision makers, from nonprofit association and education executives; board members; event staff and volunteers; other professional auctioneers; and event planners, are potential clients. By spending high quality time with me I can naturally and easily cultivate those relationships for future business.

Conducting your own seminars is fantastic fertile ground for you to develop and deliver new material to a very warm audience that is hungry for you, and your ideas and cogent content. You get closer to your clients and learn what they care about, and how you can provide custom solutions. I have not found a better way to cultivate those one-on-one connections.

Again, you will generate new revenue streams from selling these new products at your own seminars. Always record every presentation and seminar so you can easily create fresh products. And the most exciting seminar merit is creating a very loyal referral network and receiving exuberant participant testimonials. Capture video testimonials on your smart phone in the moment and, with permission, put them on your website.

꒰ *Brilliant Quick Tip* ꒱

Conducting your own seminars is fertile ground for you to develop and deliver new material to a very warm audience.

3. Give Back: *Inspire Others and Yourself*

Would you be willing to consider the possibility of giving back to your community for something you deeply love? If you are new to this concept, or if you'd like to have greater impact, here are some ideas. Select a cause that impassions you. Check the cause out on their website; call them up and talk to staff and volunteers. Get involved in a way that's meaningful for you. You could volunteer at an event or special program, you could serve on a committee or the board, you could even make a contribution if you are inspired.

You'll meet wonderful like-minded people, make friends, build a network of business allies, learn new things, empower your self-confidence, enjoy yourself, and most importantly, support something you really care about that help others. Best of all, you'll feel really good too, and when you feel confident and positive, you'll attract more positivity and greatness into your life.

⋛ *Brilliant Quick Tip* ⋚

*Get involved in a cause that's meaningful
to you. You'll meet wonderful people,
build a network of business allies,
empower and enjoy yourself, and
support something that helps others.*

I created The Kingston Fund as a memorial tribute to my parents and to provide a unique opportunity for my nephew and seven nieces to learn how philanthropy works from the inside. All eight comprise our Board of Advisors. We hold our annual Kingston Fund meeting on Thanksgiving, between turkey and pumpkin pie, where they discuss needs of charities and decide funding for our annual grants to help abused kids, hospice, and families in need.

Kathy's Call-to-Action

Give tremendous value; delight your audiences and your clients. The benefits to you are plentiful: helping participants with your valuable expertise, and thrilling loyal clients who will be delighted to refer you time and again. You'll leverage your position as a thought leader in your industry and create a highly profitable income stream for your speaking business, so you can enjoy working anywhere in the world and take your life back with more freedom and discretionary time.

From that rainy day dry cleaner inspirational sign, to John Wiley and Sons, Inc. publishing my first book, I've profited by these same vital strategies. What about you?

How will you showcase your unique talents, insights, and expertise by writing, teaching, and giving back to catapult your speaking business and to publish your book?

I wish you unprecedented success and I'm inspired to help you create your own economy. Please feel free to contact me and share your ideas.

About Kathy Kingston

An award winning speaker, author, and consultant, Kathy Kingston is the pre-eminent expert in fundraising auctions, having raised millions of dollars across the country. More than a professional auctioneer, Kathy is a "professional asker" who teaches people how to successfully and confidently ask for money. Her entertaining style and her innovative strategies motivate audiences to break revenue records. Kathy once sold a tangerine for $2,500. Her new book, *A Higher Bid,* published by John Wiley and Sons, Inc. will be released mid 2015.

Learn more about Kathy Kingston at:
HowToRaiseMoreMoney.com

21

≳Brilliant Advice≲
from Liz Uram

The Keys to Being Memorable:
Engagement, Preparation, and Confidence

Think about some of the best speakers you've heard. What was it that made them so memorable? What did they do? What did they say? How did they make you feel? When I teach a class on presentation skills, I always start by asking these questions and the same three things always top the list: audience engagement, speaker preparation, and speaker confidence. Your audience wants the same things that you want.

Engagement

Audiences aren't content to just sit and listen. They want to be part of the experience. Involvement can take a variety of forms, from simply hearing their name, to answering questions, to participating in an activity. An audience waiting in anticipation of hearing their name or of having the chance to answer a question or participate in an activity, is an engaged audience.

The sweetest word to everyone's ears is their own name. In the classic self-help book *How to Win Friends & Influence People*, Dale Carnegie lists calling other people by name as one of the top six ways to get people to like you. As a speaker, getting people to like you is highly desirable. Just imagine a room full of people eagerly waiting to hear their name. They certainly won't be nodding off or checking their cell phones. You can use this technique in any setting big or small if you make a point of it. If you're speaking to a large crowd you can make a point of meeting a few people ahead of time or you can ask their names during your presentation. If you are speaking to a smaller group, make a point of introducing yourself to people as they come in. You'll win them over from the very start and that makes the rest of your job easier. I can't tell you how many events I've attended where the speaker was standing right by the door and didn't make any effort to make contact. Needless to say, they missed an opportunity to make a great first impression.

> ⋛ *Brilliant Quick Tip* ⋚
>
> *Calling people by name is a fantastic way to engage members of your audience.*

People love the opportunity to show off their knowledge, and asking questions is a great way to get your audience involved. This technique comes with a warning—it takes strong facilitation skills for audience participation to work. You can quickly lose control of your audience and get thrown off balance if you don't maintain control of the room. Manage questions carefully so you don't lose control. If someone tries to ask a question that you aren't prepared to answer, or if answering it will move you off track, simply respond that you will allow time for questions at the end, or that you will be available after the session for questions if that is the case. If your facilitation skills aren't strong you can ask rhetorical questions. A rhetorical question is one that doesn't require an answer. It's used to make a point or get the audience to think about something. Rhetorical questions are also useful if you aren't sure of the mood of your audience. There's nothing more awkward than asking a question and getting silence in return. Use the question technique with the person's name for a winning combination. You're more likely to get a response if you call out a specific person.

Use activities to get the audience involved; it can be as simple as an individual writing exercise, an activity with a partner, or a group activity that requires moving around. As with asking questions, only use the partner and group activity techniques if you have strong facilitation skills or you risk losing control of the room.

Whether or not you use activities can depend on a variety of factors, such as the nature of your presentation, the length of your talk, and the audience size. A keynote presentation is usually short and inspirational and does not allow a lot of time for activities. If you are presenting a breakout session or workshop that is an hour or more in duration, it's important to build in time for activities to keep the audience alert and interested.

For example, when I teach a three-hour workshop, I strive to follow a thirty to seventy ratio of lecture to activities. That equates to thirty-five minutes of activities for every fifty-minute segment. That may seem like a lot but your audience will appreciate it. Finally, select activities for optimal interaction based on the size of the room. Clusters of five to six work well for large groups. Partner activities work well for small groups. Be sure to have a way to regain everyone's attention when the time is up. Flashing the lights in the room or raising your hand work well.

Engagement Action Tips:

⋛ Make a point of introducing yourself to the audience and learn a few names ahead of time that you can use throughout your presentation. Try to have at least three names to draw from.

⋛ Create a list of questions, rhetorical or actual, that you can ask during your presentation.

⋛ Use a variety of activities to keep your audience involved. Create a library of activities to have available so you can use the right one for the right occasion.

Preparation

Audiences want a prepared presenter. It shows that they care, it demonstrates knowledge of the topic, and it's what the audience expects. Preparedness can be shown in a multitude of ways, from arriving on time, to having handouts ready, to delivering a presentation with a smooth flow. If your goal is to get referrals and testimonials, it's important to present yourself as a professional, and one of the things that separates the professional from the amateur is preparation.

⋛ *Brilliant Quick Tip* ⋜

If your goal is to gain referrals and testimonials, and to show up as a respected professional, be prepared.

Rushing in at the last minute is not professional. Arrive early enough to get a feel for the room and your speaking area. Meet your host and get a lay of the land. Give yourself time to check out the technology and make sure everything works. Save yourself some stress and don't wait until your designated start time to find out that your audio/visual needs won't be met. A professional always brings their own tools, so bring your own laptop and mic if you need one. After the logistics are taken care of you can settle in, breathe, do your power pose, and you'll be ready to take command of the room.

If you are providing handouts, be sure they look professional and bring enough for everyone. A copy of your PowerPoint is okay but it's not great; a separate handout is better. Speaking of PowerPoint, the old ways don't cut it anymore. Less is more when it comes to slides and no one will listen to you if they can read your presentation on the screen. Replace text with images and use your speaking skills to paint a picture around the images. Get rid of any clip art; it's outdated. You can find all the images you need to make a brilliant presentation on the Internet. Just search Google images. Get creative and find images that illustrate your point instead of spelling it out in text-heavy slides. If you do use text in your slides, use bullet points and keep it simple. You can include bullet points on your handouts to support your main topics.

Practice delivering your presentation so your flow is smooth. Consider separating your speech into timed segments to keep an even pace and avoid spending too much time on any one area and not enough in another. A presentation that is loosely structured around your main points will allow for flexibility in the event you want to invite audience participation. On the flip side, don't be so rigid and scripted that you freeze if you forget a line. If you do forget a line, don't draw attention to it. No one knows but you. Do your best to prepare and don't beat yourself up if it isn't as perfect as you'd like. You will have plenty of opportunities to work on perfecting your performance. The best place to practice is on stage or at the front of the room, so your main objective needs to be finding those opportunities so you can keep improving. Evaluate yourself after each performance, be honest about what you can do better, and work on those areas. You'll improve with every attempt.

A quick note about audience evaluations: don't take them personally—either good or bad—and only focus on trends, not one outlier with a bad opinion.

Preparation Action Tips

≥ Arrive early. Check to make sure your equipment is set up properly and works as expected. Get comfortable in your surroundings.

≥ Provide professional looking handouts. Don't become PowerPoint dependent; keep it simple and remember that PowerPoint is a support tool, not the main event.

≥ Practice, practice, practice. Use an outline for timing and structure but allow for flexibility.

Confidence

Audience members want the person speaking to be confident. Confidence can mask a lot of minor mistakes.

Things happen. The show must go on—even when there are technology failures or other snafus. Have you ever seen a speaker fall to pieces because their presentation wouldn't load? It isn't a pretty sight. A speaker who makes a fuss and gets thrown off kilter because things didn't go as planned will lose their audience right from the start. Don't point out your mistakes. Your audience doesn't know what you forgot to say or bring. A confident presenter can carry on regardless of what goes wrong.

"How do I have more confidence?" That's one of the biggest questions I get when I teach a workshop on presentation skills. The secret to having more confidence is acting as if you *are* confident.

In her 2012 *TED Talk,* "Your Body Language Shapes Who You Are," Amy Cuddy talks about the importance of body language when it comes to confidence. She suggests using power poses to increase your confidence when faced with an intimidating situation. A power pose is a stance you take that makes you feel powerful. It could be putting your feet up on a desk with your hands behind your head; or standing like Wonder Woman with chin held high, hands on hips, and feet apart. You can adopt your power pose when driving your car simply by sitting up straight and putting one arm around the passenger seat. The pose doesn't matter, what matters is how it makes you feel. Once you decide on your power pose, get into position and hold it for a full two minutes. At the end of two minutes you will feel invincible and prepared to take on the world. While some of the more overt poses are meant to be done in private, you can adopt a more subtle pose such as sitting up straight and holding your chin up in public and no one will know except you.

Body language, voice, and eye contact are all factors you can control that can make you look more confident than you feel. Your audience has no idea how you feel, they only know how you make them feel. The more confident you appear, the more comfortable you'll make them feel. In addition to doing your power pose ahead of time, there are a few body language tips to keep in mind during your presentation. Walk in like you own the room and take command with your presence. Stand up straight, shoulders back, and chin up. Move around within your speaking area, don't pace or shift from one foot to the other. When you speak, use a clear, loud voice; rarely will people say anything if they can't hear you. They would rather sit through a garbled presentation unable to hear the presenter than speak up.

ꞓ *Brilliant Quick Tip* ꞓ

Take command with your presence;
walk in like you own the room.

But that's okay, it's your job to ask them. Use a mic if you need one. I know a presenter who has a portable mic and speaker that he uses even in small classrooms because his voice doesn't carry in the least and people need to hear him.

Don't forget to make eye contact with your audience. Scan the room and hit as many people as possible.

Confidence Action Tips

- ꞓ Don't point out your mistakes. No one else knows but you what you meant to say or do.

- ꞓ Adopt a power pose and get in the habit of holding it for about two minutes before show time to increase your confidence.

⋛ Demonstrate confidence through your walk and talk when you're in front of the room.

Following these simple steps will help you quickly develop into a professional speaker. However, it's one thing to read about it and another thing to do it. The real magic and real improvement happens when you're on the stage or in front of the room. So get out there, do your best, and keep moving forward!

About Liz Uram

Liz Uram is the owner of The Coach & Mentor Group. She is an a an award-winning speaker and highly regarded trainer and facilitator who delivers innovative and engaging training programs to business professionals.

Liz specializes in leadership skills, organizational development, performance feedback, as well as strategic planning. With over fifteen years of corporate and entrepreneurial experience, Liz brings a wealth of relevant and practical information to her clients. She is also the co-host of a popular weekly podcast, The Focus Radio.

Learn more about Liz Uram at:
CoachAndMentor.net

22

≷Brilliant Advice≷
from Elizabeth Quintanilla

A Lesson for Business Owners Who Use
Speaking as a Marketing Strategy

Everyone thinks they can do public speaking, particularly as a form of marketing. However, we often work with (or hear from) CEOs and VPs of sales who say they wish speaking—as a form of marketing—was better for them than it actually is.

We admire great speakers and marketers. When we think of the great marketers, top of mind are Coke, Southwest Airlines, and Apple. What makes them great? They are memorable and combine their story with their brand promise.

Let's begin our lesson with storytelling. My life is a story, as all of our lives actually are. That's good to remember when you think about speaking as a form of marketing.

When we hear a good story, our minds often visualize the setting, sounds, smells, and perhaps even the tastes we relate to in the story.

My secret sauce to a marketing speech is taking a little bit of heart and a sprinkle of sass (in careful measurements), and remembering all of my mother's bits of wisdom—while stirring.

When I was growing up, we had multiple Christmas dinners. Our immediate family celebrated the holidays early with a turkey dinner, and we didn't have to save the leftovers before leaving to see our cousins to eat turkey again. As a kid, it was always more fun to eat my cousin's leftovers on vacation than it was to reheat my own at home, to make a turkey sandwich!

Now pause . . . what did your mind just visualize when you read the previous story? Was it relatable? Did you visualize your childhood kitchen or your cousin's kitchen? Did it bring a warm, fuzzy feeling about Christmas?

A carefully crafted message requires that you consider the perspective of your audience in terms of what is compelling to them. Then you must use that to persuade them to take action.

Following is the definition of the word *persuasion* according to BusinessDictionary.com:

> *Process aimed at changing a person's (or a group's) attitude or behavior toward some event, idea, object, or other person(s), by using written or spoken words to convey information, feelings, or reasoning, or a combination of them.*

When speaking as a form of marketing, be sure to be persuasive in your messaging and inspire your audience to take an action.

⪼ *Brilliant Quick Tip* ⪻

In your marketing speeches, be persuasive with your message and inspire your audience to take an action.

Master marketers know how to wield their influence with carefully crafted messages, and persuade society through them.

When was the last time you ordered a "pop?" In fact, when asked by a waitress what we would like to drink, many of us in Texas (where I live) ask for a Coke. The waitress will then ask if we want a sprite, root beer, or a Coke. This just goes to show who has our brain in the sugary beverage category!

We are now influenced in our daily culture by advertising, news, mass media, and politics. Therefore, master marketers recommend that we incorporate a practice of persuasion in our marketing tool kit.

Think Like a Marketer

The following is my favorite description of marketing:

> *"If the circus is coming to town and you paint a sign saying 'Circus Coming to the Fairground Saturday,' that's advertising. If you put the sign on the back of an elephant and walk it into town, that's promotion. If the elephant walks through the mayor's flower bed, that's publicity. And if you get the mayor to laugh about it, that's public relations. If the town's citizens go to the circus, and buy tickets, that's sales. If you actually intended for all this to happen, that's marketing!"*

> –Attributed to P.T. Barnum, with the author of the last line unknown.

Most engineers new to marketing want to talk about the *features* that make the shiny new object they are taking to the market, special. By discussing features, they *try* to make their product seem exciting to new customers. However, most consumers want the "why" of the product; in other words, the "what it does for me."

For example, an engineer will market a drill bit as:

Masonry Multi-construction, Multi-purpose Drill Bit, 50 x 85 mm, d 5 mm

A marketer would describe the same drill bit as:

Bosch Daredevil Long Life Bit Set Replacement Drill Bit, 50x 85 mm, d 5 mm

They are the same drill bit but the marketer would keep your attention longer and include the benefit of this drill bit: a long lasting (long life), not going to have to replace anytime soon, for your do-it-yourself (Daredevil) projects.

Here is an example of persuasive writing from a Bosch drill bit featured on Amazon:

This Bosch 1-inch by 16-inch flute by 21-inch SDS max rotary hammer drill bit offers improved performance with its carbide-tipped head with four cutting edges. The bit is designed to help reduce vibration when drilling. The bit shaft wears at a slower rate and better withstands repeated use.

The above example is all about the "why"—*why* does the target audience need what you are offering? When preparing your content for a presentation, be sure to write in terms of your customer's "why" or "what's in it for me." If you want to use speaking to market your products, then in your message, subtlety include the important benefits that will influence your customer on why your product/program/service is more valuable than other, similar options.

꒰ *Brilliant Quick Tip* ꒱

If speaking is your way to market products, then when preparing your message, write in terms of your customer's "why." Include the benefits that will influence your customer to choose your product over other options.

We are always competing for "brain space" in the minds of our customers. They are often distracted with other thoughts, from their need to pick up the kids from school later in the day, to preparing that next PowerPoint presentation for an upcoming sales meeting. As speakers and marketers, we must answer our customers' objections before we ever have a chance to meet, so that when they attend our speech, we can easily cut through their thought-clutter.

Most consumers are inclined to say "*No.*" It's not personal; perhaps it is just that most of us are too distracted in our everyday lives to think critically about every option that is being shown to us. Therefore, we must continually practice addressing our customers' objections by incorporating the benefits—their "why"—into our marketing speeches.

One of my favorite marketing lessons on delivering your carefully crafted persuasive message—the one that has been painstakingly written for the perspective of your customer—is from *Singing in the Rain*. In this scene, our supporting male actor teaches our leading man a little lesson to make his life better. Here are selected portions of the *lyrics:

Though the world is so full of a number things,
I know we should all be as happy as
But are we?
No, definitely no, positively no.
Decidedly no. Mm mm

And in the words of that immortal buddy
Samuel J. Snodgrass, as he was about to be lead
To the guillotine:

Make 'em laugh
Don't you know everyone wants to laugh?
(Ha ha!)

My grandpa said go out and tell 'em a joke
But give it plenty of hoke
Make 'em roar
Make 'em scream

Make 'em laugh
Don't you know everyone wants to laugh?
Ah ha ha ha ha ha ha

(*Song Tile: "Make 'Em Laugh." Written by Arthur Freed and Nacio Herb Brown. Performed by Donald O'Connor.)

How do you keep your customer's attention in a noisy world? The quote: "Make 'em laugh" is just as true today as it was over fifty years ago when Gene Kelly wore his dancing shoes.

Perhaps you remember the Old Spice commercial where a sexy man was going through a number of funny situations, and you actually watched the commercial just to laugh. This situational comedy still exists. You may have also enjoyed the "Don't Touch My Dart" commercials featuring a well-known comedian and his annoying neighbor. Part of being memorable is leaving a favorable impression, and laughter is a subtle way of persuading someone to "like" you just a little bit more than they may have without the laughter.

A Personal Brand

Many of the same principles that work well for corporate branding of products and services also work for personal branding. I choose to be a marketing gunslinger so I can stand out as a distinct choice; the market has options, and my potential clients can choose a number of marketing consultants with a variety of backgrounds, so I want to stand out. How do you stand out? By choosing a distinct (and succinct) visually descriptive positioning statement that leaves the potential customer asking for more!

Personal branding is just as valuable as the branding of a consumer-packaged product. In fact, the 2014 season cast of *Dancing with the Stars* featured for the first time, a YouTube star who became influential as a high school student, sharing her tips and point of view from her bedroom.

Perhaps you are rolling your eyes, but wonder why this is important to illustrate. First, do you know what your kids are watching on their laptops or tablets? Who influences their behavior? Have you noticed that teen fashion magazines are thinner today than they were when you were younger?

The producers of *Dancing with the Stars* were eager to inject new energy into a hit series that's been on TV since 2005. So, they recruited Bethany Mota, an eighteen-year-old fashion icon whose YouTube channel boasts more than seven million subscribers. Ms. Mota, who teaches her fans how to decorate their rooms, style their hair, or pick the right accessory, is the first star from Google's video site to be cast on the show. Additionally, she was recently part of a YouTube campaign where her image was associated with the following slogan: *"You make confidence THE must-have accessory."*

There are several other fashion teen vloggers (YouTube video bloggers) that could have been picked. Let's analyze another fashion and beauty guru.

Have you heard of Blair Fowler? If you have a teenager, she may be watching Blair's "Haul" videos, in which the vlogger goes through shopping bags from a variety of stores, detailing the latest finds for her audience. She keeps a focused message on fashion insights and beauty how-tos. Her videos have over sixty-one million views: a fashion marketer's dream come true.

In advertising, marketers quite often pay for "number of impressions" online, and sometimes that is quite expensive, especially for a generic keyword such as "fashion." However, entrepreneurial teenagers are finding ways to successfully build an audience by accepting advertising on their YouTube channel as well as by gathering sponsorships from brands they enjoy. After all, teenagers are much more likely to relate to another teen than to yet another marketing executive.

This is an influential relationship, because it may be a great marketing strategy to equip your biggest fans with the tools and scripts to share your story. Are you making it easy for your raving customers to talk about you, before or after they see you on the stage?

Branding is not something you create in isolation. It is the impression others have about you based on several factors, including your messaging and what people say about you. Your brand is the sum of many conversations and interactions, so seek ways to continually leverage your influential relationships.

≳ *Brilliant Quick Tip* ≲

Equip your biggest fans with the tools to share your story. Make it easy for them to talk about you before and after they see you on the stage. Find ways to leverage your influential relationships.

We are the brand-keepers, and like a chess master, we have to be thinking two to five steps ahead to keep putting our best foot forward. Have a strong message, and empower your fans on as many mediums as possible (that still make sense to them) so they can share your best brand stories in a relatable way.

Opportunities Must Meet with Hard Work

Are you paying attention when opportunities knock? There are very few overnight successes and lots of behind the scenes hard work.

Did you realize that the CEO of Duck Commander, Willie Robinson, was first seen as an applicant on *The Amazing Race*? As a fan of the show *Duck Dynasty*, I enjoy watching a family that actually likes each other. How did the show get started?

Willie was known to buy candy at Wal-Mart and sell it to his classmates (pre-YouTube), and he is a master marketer worth watching. While Phil and Jase perfected the duck call (the shiny object they sold as engineers), Willie, the risk-taking younger brother, made the product explode with partnerships from shotgun companies, shell companies, and camouflage manufacturers. He leveraged well-known influencers such as the Washington Nationals first baseman Adam LaRoche, and country stars Jason Aldean and Luke Bryan. Under Willie, TV opportunities arose, and he became the executive producer of their two shows on the Outdoor Channel, *Duck Commander* and *Buck Commander*.

A master marketer is open to new opportunities and jumps, regardless of the risk or of appearing foolish. Remember to put yourself out there, and not just as an avatar on Twitter or a resume on LinkedIn.

Follow-Up

The final master marketing tip in our lesson for speakers is to follow-up. Be sure to follow through with the organization that invited you to speak.

About Elizabeth Quintanilla

Elizabeth Quintanilla is a positive, creative, people-oriented, and performance-driven Marketing Gunslinger. She is a collaborator, communicator, and speaker with a focus on understanding the customer perspective. She consults on a variety of topics, including online technologies and strategies, social business, management, and marketing (online, social, content, traditional, product, and go-to-market). As an expert consultant, she effectively simplifies complex concepts while delivering high-quality, creative solutions to ensure success.

Elizabeth actively serves as on the Austin Community Technology and Telecommunications Commission.

Learn more about Elizabeth Quintanilla at: MarketingGunslingers.com

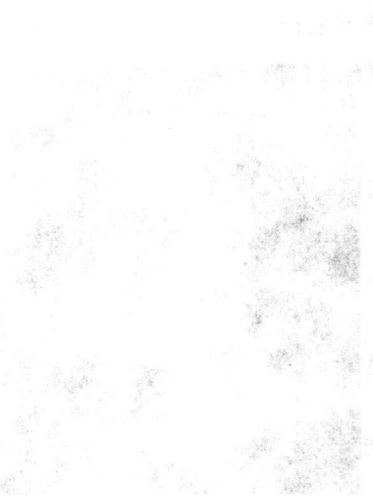

23

⸘Brilliant Advice⸎
from Bruce Keith

A 90% Speaker or 10% Speaker?

Having been in the business of selling and speaking in excess of forty years, one truth continues to dominate my thinking. Regardless of what business you are in or regardless of what you do on a daily basis, you are always selling. It starts when you are a small child and it never stops. It starts with, *"Can I have another cookie?"* and continues throughout the rest of your life. Selling is certainly part of being a powerful speaker. When you are on stage—no matter what your message—you are communicating information, ideas, possibilities, inspiration, etc. and you want your audience to buy into your message. The bottom line is that you want your audience to leave with something more than they brought with them. As a speaker, your job is to provide added value so they will "come back for more." When you accomplish that goal, you are a "10% Speaker."

The concept of "90% or 10%" comes from a great insight I learned from business philosopher Jim Rohn, who was an amazing speaker himself. Jim said *"In my experience, for most seminars, 90% of the audience takes great notes, takes them home, and does nothing with them. Conversely, the other 10% go home with the same information and make dramatic changes in their lives."* I have used this quote as a speaker numerous times. It's a great way to get your audience to concentrate more on your message and not drift off. Then one day the "message behind the message" struck me like the high beams from an oncoming car in the middle of the night—there was a powerful lesson in Mr. Rohn's quote for me as a speaker. Didn't I have a responsibility here too? Wasn't it also up to me to make sure that my audience members were always in the 10% group? I decided then and there that I would buckle down and be completely responsible for providing that level of impactful information from the stage. Sometimes when speaking I am selling information and sometimes I'm selling products. Regardless, I'm always selling. My job is to sell them on doing something differently as a result of my message. It's up to me to be sure that everyone in the room is in the 10% group. My job is to make sure that I'm always a "10% Speaker". . . never a "90% Speaker"!

So How to Do That?

How do I do that? How do I set myself apart from every other speaker so they will "keep coming back for more"? When you think about those two questions, it is critical for you to understand that being a great speaker is a learned skill. Focus on that idea for a moment; everyone can learn how to master the 10% challenge. It's safe to say that legendary orators like Martin Luther King Jr., Elizabeth I, and Abraham Lincoln were born with some of the talents they exhibited. At the same time, to be really compelling in communicating a message from the stage requires practice, study, and a lot of effort. Don't think that Martin Luther King Jr. didn't work on refining his incredible communication style. Speaking powerfully takes a lot of skill. The good news is this skill can be developed over time. There's lots of trial and error involved. I've lost count of the number of mistakes I've made from the stage. I do know that the commitment to not making the same mistake twice is a great way to get better every time. What follows are my top three techniques for making sure that as a speaker your audience is in the 10% group—the group that leaves with significantly more than they came with. Here are three guaranteed strategies that will set you apart from the rest and help you take your presentations and your confidence level to a whole new height, almost immediately. Enjoy . . .

Guaranteed Strategy #1: *Tell Stories—Lots of Stories*

The best speakers are masters at engaging their audiences right from the beginning of their presentation. Engaging your audience in your message is a critical aspect of a successful talk. By far the most powerful way to engage your audience is to tell stories. Mankind has been communicating through the spoken word for centuries. Storytelling was the way the best communicators connected with their listeners. Think of the people from early civilization sitting around the campfire repeating what had gone on that day so everyone was up to speed on the basic need of survival. When the written word was introduced, many of the first pages that were created were stories. The Bible is completely full of stories and parables that communicate a message. And so it is today—storytelling humanizes the message and creates a more intimate sense of involvement for the listener.

When building your talk, be sure to include as many stories as possible to help "sell" your point. For example, let's say you wanted to describe how critical it is to be able to deal with adversity in life and in business. You could tell the story about Steve Jobs getting fired from Apple at age thirty and then coming back a few years later, to make it into the largest and most profitable company in the world. You could talk about how he shared his story of dealing with adversity at his now famous Commencement Address at Sanford University in 2005. Even those who have heard the story will become engaged and involved again in the power of how he dealt with all the challenges, and came out on top. Everyone loves a winner. Every story needs a hero. In the Apple story—Steve Jobs is a hero. In this case, the topic was adversity . . . the story makes it real.

In his bestseller, *Tell to Win*, media executive Peter Gruber shares how to "Connect, Persuade, and Triumph with the Hidden Power of Story." Author Annette Simmons writes an equally fascinating overview on storytelling entitled, *Whoever Tells the Best Story Wins*. Annette's message is all about "How to Use Your Own Stories to Communicate with Power and Impact." The next time you are listening to a great presenter, pay attention to their use of stories to get their message across; stories of inspiration, stories of pain and sorrow, stories of victory, stories of hope, etc. They all engage the audience. Take note of how involved you become and how you feel part of the story they are telling. Stories take the concept of a message and make it visual in your imagination. Stories paint pictures and bring the listener right into the action. This approach will do the same for your audience. By the way, there is a terrific side benefit here. Everyone loves to tell stories . . . it will help you build enthusiasm for your message in the same way it engages your audience!

Start collecting stories right now. Create a folder in your computer or in your desk drawer and start building up your inventory of great stories. Don't worry about where you would use them or how you would use them. Just start accumulating. When you are preparing your next presentation, pull two or three out from the folder and sprinkle them throughout your talk. This strategy is surprisingly easy and amazingly effective. Tell stories—lots of stories.

Ξ *Brilliant Quick Tip* Ξ

Be a story collector; start building up your inventory of great stories you can share with audiences. When preparing your next presentation, sprinkle a few of them throughout your talk.

Guaranteed Strategy #2: *Give Them Hope*

When you offer hope to your audience, they will listen much more intently. Remember that no matter what your message from the stage, you are always selling. Even if you are a lecturer at a university, you are selling. The university professor is selling knowledge—he/she wants their students to learn new information and concepts and then use that knowledge to help them move forward in their learning process. If it is presented in a boring fashion, then the chance of absorbing that knowledge decreases. In becoming a powerful speaker, the concept of "Giving Them Hope" is all about showing the audience what is possible. It's the opposite of boring.

This is a critical point: when you are showing someone what is possible, you are giving them hope. The hope is that they can use this information to their advantage. To become a great speaker the challenge is to be able to help your audience see how they can transform your ideas into real life results. Hope in itself is of little value—unless you do something with it. As retired NCAA football coach Woody Hayes said, *"Hope is not a strategy."* So how do you take your audience past the level of having new ideas to actually using them to their advantage? How do you help them make that transition?

The solution is to give them specific *action steps* that are doable and easy to follow. Now your message has gone from information (what to do) to hope (how to do it). The 90% speaker only shows the audience *what to do*. The 10% speaker shows the audience *how to do it*. One of the products I sell to my audiences from the stage is called "All the Right Words." It is a large collection of scripts and dialogs for real estate salespeople to use in communication with their prospects and customers. I learned very quickly that simply making these scripts and dialogues available to my audience was not sufficient. Here's why . . . just knowing the words was only the *what to say* part. I was missing the "hope factor." As a speaker, what I had to do was *demonstrate* the delivery of these words. They had to *hear and feel* how to communicate these words in a comfortable and conversational fashion. This is the *how to say it* part. They had to believe that *they* could do the same.

So we created a series of six specific *action steps* on *how* to deliver the message to their customers in a compelling fashion. I began demonstrating to the audience how to take the words and humanize their delivery. These *action steps* showed what was possible for every single person in the audience. This is the "Give Them Hope" part. The rest of the story is this: our sales volume took off and dramatically more people invested in the "All the Right Words" product immediately. Lesson learned: it's not enough to show them what to do, you have to show them *how* to do it. We even added a "how-to" DVD to our offering to make sure that the *action steps* were always present.

⋛ *Brilliant Quick Tip* ⋚

Give your audience members the hope that they can use the information you share in their own lives; offer them specific, easy-to-follow action steps.

Make sure your audience leaves your session with an enthusiastic mindset that says *"I can do this,"* or *"I can use this information,"* or *"This isn't complicated, we can start using this information right away."* Make it easy for them; give them *action steps* and you will *give them hope.*

Guaranteed Strategy #3: *Be You*

One of the best pieces of advice I ever got when I started my speaking business was the following, *"Bruce, just be yourself. Don't try to be anyone else, don't try to be like so-and-so, just be you. You are fine the way you are. Work at honing your skills and improving your delivery and you will be very successful."* Guess what? They were right. For a long time, I had been guilty of doing the opposite. I can remember as a young boy watching the Sunday morning evangelists on TV, and marveling at how they did things. They knew how to speak loudly and then softly, they knew how and when to pause, some could even cry on demand; they had it all! It was the same with watching superstars like Larry King and Katie Couric, and sportscasters like Curt Gowdy and Bob Costas. I figured, if I could just be like those people, I'd be a great speaker. Sounds okay, but obviously that's impossible. The better advice is to observe the top professionals and then work on your strengths using some of their techniques where applicable.

Following are some of my favorite "be you" ideas that you can incorporate without changing who you are. That way you'll just be focusing on your strengths.

Don't Lecture

Don't lecture and don't talk down—just have a conversation with your audience. Most of the time it will be a one-way conversation, and that's just fine. Regardless, talk to them the way you would talk to a friend whom you haven't seen for some time. We've all seen speakers who seem to be on a power trip. They start off just fine and end up alienating everyone by trying to impress them with how much they know. Leadership guru John C. Maxwell is an expert at connecting with his audience. He is a former preacher who has mastered the technique of laughing at himself and seemingly chatting with a room filled with thousands of people. John's secret is his ego is not out of control.

Ask Lots of Questions

Rhetorical questions—sprinkle lots of questions throughout your talk. You are not looking for people to interrupt you and answer these questions; just remember they will be much more engaged when they feel you are speaking to them. For example, "*By a show of hands, how many of you have already experienced what I just described?*"

Use Humor

Use humor, but just make sure it's your own personal type of humor. If you are not a joke teller, then don't tell jokes. Here's a simple barometer to use: when you share the things that you find funny, then you are using your humor at its best. If you are laughing, then your audience will be laughing. Sometimes, it's simply a humorous phrase or a quick anecdote that will get the laugh you are looking for; it's another very effective way of engaging your audience. One final point that should never escape you: keep it clean . . . squeaky clean.

Energy Level

It is hugely important that you exhibit a strong energy level from the stage. Here's where "being you" is a bit tricky. Of course, you don't want to come across as someone who is wildly manic—like Jim Carrey in one of his out-of-control scenes (such as in *Dumb and Dumber*). There's a fine line. Here are a couple of guidelines: if you are naturally expressive then you don't need to ramp it up much. If you are relatively low-key you probably need to add some "jump" to your game. Remember this: whoever you are in "real-life," you should come across as being *energetic* from the stage. It feels like you are being "a little over the top" then surprisingly, that's probably about the right amount to project. When you think about a boring politician making a speech, you understand what I mean about the other side of that coin. Don't go there! Take special care to watch your audience—make sure they are engaged. If you see them "dozing off" then increase the energy you are projecting immediately.

> ⋛ *Brilliant Quick Tip* ⋚
>
> *In terms of your energy level on stage, if you're naturally expressive then you don't need to ramp it up much. If you're relatively low-key you probably need to add some "jump" to your game.*

Who Do They See?

Make sure you are presenting yourself visually in the way you want to be perceived. When you walk on stage, before you even open your mouth, your audience has formed an opinion of who you are. It's that fast! If you create the wrong impression right off the bat, it's hard to turn that around! You will spend the first few minutes of your talk "pushing a rock up a hill" if you present the wrong image. I have a speaker friend who does not dress his best because, "*I want them to see me as a regular guy who they can relate to.*" The problem is, the "regular guy" he's trying to portray does not come across as being very impressive. Make sure you are showing them the professional in you that you want them to see. While it's important to "be you," just make sure that it's the BEST YOU they get to see.

Wrapping Up

When you are on stage, make sure that you come across exhibiting the *you* who is relaxed, enthusiastic, natural, and most of all committed to your audience's success. I can remember preparing for a presentation many years ago and saying to myself, *"When I get up there I'm going to be amazing!"* Guess what? I wasn't amazing! It was forced and unnatural. I had to learn to relax and enjoy myself. Once I started following that approach, I was well on my way to becoming a 10% speaker.

Here are a couple of questions that will help you make that transition. First of all, you need to do an "out of body" experience while you are performing and subconsciously ask yourself, *"Who am I being right now?"* Naturally, you want the answer to be a positive reflection of the way you want to be perceived. The second question is a fun question to ask yourself all the time. It is, *"Would I buy from me right now?"* You already know you are up there selling—you are selling your message to your audience. If your answer is *"Yes,"* and if you would "buy from me right now," then your audience will do the same. The bottom line is, if it feels right for you then no doubt you are doing the right things. Take on these ideas and incorporate them into who you are and who you can be. *Be a 10% speaker . . . tell stories, give them hope, and be you.* Enjoy the journey!

About Bruce Keith

Bruce Keith is a leading motivational speaker and trainer for sales organizations in North America, specializing in real estate sales. He has been in real estate in excess of twenty-five years, the last fifteen or more as a sales coach, speaker, and trainer. His organization helps sales professionals grow their business rapidly using down to earth, easy to implement sales techniques and strategies. His high energy couple with his "No Excuses Accountability" approach has helped thousands increase their production significantly.

Learn more about Bruce Keith at:
BruceKeithResults.com

24

﹩Brilliant Advice﹩
from Shirley Dalton

The S.M.A.R.T. Speaker

Inspirational and motivational speaker Les Brown says, "*You don't have to be great to get started, but you do have to get started to be great.*"

I love this quote. In fact, I love lots of quotes, because they remind me of the things I need to believe or do in order to get where I want to go.

My passion in life is personal development; mine and everybody else's.

I love learning; I can't help myself.

I love teaching.

Sometimes, we learn from what others teach us. Sometimes we learn by observation, and sometimes we learn the hard way through experience or trial and error. The following tips are tips I wish someone had shared with me when I was first starting to speak. If I had known then what I know now, I would have been one very S.M.A.R.T. speaker.

S.M.A.R.T. is an acronym of course, to help you remember. Here's what I learned the hard way. I trust it will help save you time and money on your speaking journey.

Strategy

"Speak wherever and whenever you can, especially when you are first starting out. Say 'Yes' to everything," is advice I don't recommend. Far too many speakers make this mistake. If you accept anything and everything, you are not being strategic, and if you want to ensure a profitable and enjoyable speaking career, you must be strategic.

Being strategic means you must be clear about why you are speaking and to whom you are speaking as well as taking control over the topics you speak about. I learned this lesson very early in my career, after realizing how much it actually cost me in time and money to accept speaking engagements that did not fit my strategy. (At the time I didn't have a strategy.)

Here's something I want you to remember: If you accept adhoc engagements you'll get adhoc results. Let me give you an example.

I was invited to speak at a breakfast for members of the local Chamber of Business in a rural town. I was asked to present on a topic that wasn't related to my business. I wasn't allowed to promote myself. I wasn't allowed to make an offer. I wasn't paid for the speaking gig. I traveled over eight hours by car to get there. It was a breakfast, so I arrived the day before and paid for accommodation and my evening meal.

The Chamber paid for breakfast, although I didn't eat because I often feel nervous prior to speaking and I don't want to perform on a full stomach—or worse, with food stuck in my teeth (especially green spinach or mushroom).

The group was friendly. They laughed at my jokes, cried in the right places, and were engaged in the activities. I managed to collect their names and email addresses in exchange for the opportunity to win one of my online programs. At the end of the presentation, I packed up and drove eight hours to get home. It wasn't long after I started my return journey that my inner critic surfaced.

"*Well, that was a waste of time, wasn't it? What did you get out of that?*" it demanded. "*It's not about me,*" I replied. "*It's about the audience and how I can add value to them.*" "*Oh, very noble, very noble, indeed. You would do well to remember that it must be a win-win, and I can't see your win in this situation.*" "*Oh be quiet.*" I didn't want to listen to my inner critic!

But it was right. I didn't want to face it. Apart from enjoying speaking to and engaging with the audience, I didn't really have a win in terms of business. I had seven hours to go. I had plenty of time to work out my speaking strategy. Here's what I came up with: ***All invitations to speak must be qualified.***

*To pass and therefore accept the invitation (to **qualify**):*

1. The gig must provide a win-win for the audience, event organizer, and me; in other words, it must be for the highest and best outcome for all concerned (that includes me). For me, a win could include:

    a. Being paid to speak

    b. Making an offer or promoting my products or services (sell from stage)

    c. Increasing my database

    d. Expanding brand awareness or increasing credibility as an expert

    e. Joint venture or affiliate opportunity

251

2. The topic must be aligned with my business objectives.

3. The audience must match my ideal client profile or avatar.

4. The gig must be profitable, i.e. must not cost me money to attend (unless it's a charity and that's a different set of qualifying questions).

5. The gig must not waste my time. In other words, is there anything else I could be doing that would be a better use of my time?

6. The speech must have the option to be recorded and used for future promotion.

7. The gig must offer me opportunities to collect and use testimonials.

From that day on, every invitation had to pass the test. There was no way I was going to get consistently hammered by my inner critic for that amount of time ever again.

Be S.M.A.R.T. with your speaking engagements. Always ensure you meet your *strategic goals* and provide for a win-win for all concerned.

Marketing

Unless you are an exceptional speaker and get invited to return every time you speak or you get booked for another gig from the first gig, you are going to need to market yourself.

I've found over the years that the speakers who get the most work are not always the best speakers—they are the best marketers.

If you're uncomfortable marketing yourself, either get over yourself or hire or outsource someone else to secure bookings for you. I'm sorry to be so blunt, but this is a really important point. It took me years to learn this and I don't want you to waste your valuable speaking opportunities.

> ## ⟫ *Brilliant Quick Tip* ⟨
>
> *Gaining speaking engagements requires marketing. If you don't like to market yourself, hire someone will.*

Here are some questions to help you develop your own marketing strategy (there's that word again).

1. For which industries, companies, or organizations would you like to speak?

2. What products or services do you have to offer and who is your ideal target audience to purchase them?

3. Which events does your ideal target audience attend?

4. How can you get on the stage at these events?

5. Who do you know who could introduce or refer you?

Your answers to the above questions will help you to create and implement your marketing strategy.

Another good tip is to create a marketing calendar so you can plot your engagements and ensure you have enough speaking opportunities to reach your revenue goals.

Affinity

Affinity is your ability to connect with your audience. The more you connect the more they will buy, and the key to connection is emotion.

You must decide what you want the audience to feel before crafting your speech. Once you know how you want them to feel and you know the outcome for the speech, you can easily choose from your repertoire of stories. (If you haven't already, make sure you record these and categorize them, so you can easily find or remember a story for each teaching point.)

> ⋛ *Brilliant Quick Tip* ⋚
>
> *In advance of crafting your speech, decide what you want your audience to feel. Build your speech around that.*

And this is a really important point to make. People love stories and they love to hear your stories more than others. They want to get to know you and understand who you are and what you stand for. The easiest way to share yourself is through your stories. A word of caution though: never make yourself the hero, and never indulge yourself by using the audience as your therapist. Choose stories that help you connect with the audience and that help them to solve their problems, or encourage or inspire them to take actions that will benefit them.

One of my points of differentiation is to use costumes and props. I love to dress up and assume a character or include plenty of props to engage the audience and give them a memento to remember me. Find what works for you and don't be afraid to be authentic and real. Your audience wants to get to know you.

Research

The two most important areas you need to research for any speech are:

1. The audience and desired outcomes

2. Evidence or examples to back up your stories—this could include current media topics; scientific, statistical, or historical evidence; or other facts and figures.

Your audience expects you to be the expert, so you must provide good content that is relevant to them and the desired outcomes.

Testimonials

Always, always, always ask for the opportunity to collect and record testimonials. Make sure you get them in a variety of ways; video, written, voice-overs, photos etc.

Testimonials can include details about your presentation, your content, how easy it is to work with you, or the outcomes for your audience. It's up to you. Decide what you want to showcase and then ask your happy clients if they would be willing to provide a testimonial.

> ⸗ *Brilliant Quick Tip* ⸗
>
> *Whenever you can, collect and record testimonials. Get them in a variety of forms, including, video, written, voice-overs, and photos.*

Make it easy for them; give them the script or the outline of what you would like them to say or write. In some cases, it might be easier if you write it and ask them to print on their letterhead and sign it for you. Be sure to boost their credibility as well and find a way to promote them. Remember to always look for the win-win.

So there you have it—my recommendations for being a S.M.A.R.T. speaker. Follow the tips and recommendations in that order. Start with your "why." Why are you speaking? What is your *strategy*? What is the outcome you want? *Market* yourself to get the gigs you want. Craft your speech to develop a relationship with your audience and develop an *affinity* with them. Be yourself and share yourself with them. *Research* your audience, their outcomes, and your content. Make sure you give them what they want. Ask for *testimonials*. A colleague of mine—who is a master salesperson—once reprimanded me,

"Shirl, don't say 'No' before the customer does." If you don't ask, the answer is always *"No."*

Whether you are just starting out as a speaker or have been speaking for a while, I wish you even more success.

I'll finish with my favorite quote of all time by English philosopher, Herbert Spencer, *"The great aim of education is not knowledge, but action."* Become a S.M.A.R.T. speaker. Become an even more successful speaker. S.M.A.R.T. speakers take their knowledge and turn it into action.

About Shirley Dalton

The only child of taxi proprietors, Shirley experienced firsthand the pain and pressure that small business owners face. Not wanting this for others, Shirley started a movement to fight for your freedom.

Shirley specializes in developing people and processes so your business works for you AND your people. She inspires, motivates, and teaches her clients how to get themselves and their businesses under control, make more money, and get more time.

Learn more about Shirley Dalton at: BusinessFreedomFighters.com

25

≷Brilliant Advice≷
from Clarissa Gatdula-Calingasan

From Aspiring Audience to Inspiring the Audience

"When your fear of heights becomes the highlight to fight,
When fighting to win becomes the strength to gain,
When gaining wisdom becomes the power to achieve,
When achieving to succeed becomes the inspiration to lead,
Then speaking to inspire is leading to WIN."

~Coach Clarissa C

Most speakers I know used to have the fear of public speaking. I was one of them; I was one of those shy kids who always hid behind mommy's skirt. I remember how I avoided conversations because of my banked insecurities in expressing my thoughts and feelings.

I recognized my weaknesses at an early age, and that was first a curse, and then eventually a blessing. I took up engineering in college, confident that hiding behind a technical career would protect me from public speaking. I was wrong. I eventually realized that if you want to succeed in life, regardless of your field, you will have to accept opportunities to speak up, either in small business meetings or in grand conferences.

If you are reading this book, then you must be determined and destined to speak up. I encourage you to reminisce how you have already conquered other fears and how you have already achieved daunting personal goals. Know that you are designed to get better and better at things you do; that includes becoming a better speaker. You are called to inspire many people to hear your messages. You are designed, destined, and called to WIN through speaking.

⋛ *Brilliant Quick Tip* ⋚

If the thought of speaking in public frightens you, seriously consider that you have already conquered other fears and achieved daunting personal goals. You can do this too!

Here are four important principles that can turbo-charge your success in life and in speaking:

1. Have Fun.

2. Do your best.

3. Be thankful and grateful.

4. Stay in faith

1. Have Fun: *Intend to Enjoy the Moment*

Happy speakers attract joyful participants. People who intend to have fun in their lives, most of the time, attract fun. Having fun at work or in any other area of your life can put you in a creative and productive mood.

People who experience fun while they are in action as speakers are:

⋛ Those who are comfortable in their own skin

⋛ Those who are familiar with the environment

⋛ Those who show up on stage prepared

⋛ Those who know their topics by heart

⋛ Those who are excited to deliver the message

⋛ Those who intend to inspire

⋛ Those who connect with the audience

⋛ Those who are willing to learn from the audience or participants

⋛ *Brilliant Quick Tip* ⋚

Have fun. Purpose to enjoy each moment.
It will make you a better speaker.

2. Do Your Best: *Win the Audience to Your Side*

Doing your best on stage can make a huge impact on your audience. They will feel you have come prepared and they will also feel respected as an audience. They will, in turn, respect you, and therefore easily connect with you. When you make a mistake, they will be more forgiving because they'll feel that you are there for them to share your very best.

Speakers who are ready to be the best they can be are:

1. Prepared to practice

2. Prepared to receive feedback

3. Responsible for knowing the appropriate topics and words to be delivered

4. Propelled by a winner's mindset

5. Generous in sharing knowledge to the audience

6. Able to connect with the audience

7. Skilled in entertaining with content

8. Intentional in delivering and inspiring wisdom

Speaking can be both terrifying and exciting. Speakers who decide to have courage on stage are intentional with their best performance.

Professional speakers are expected to present good content, narrate amusing experiences, and impart wisdom to the audience. They are expected to follow perfect flow and demonstrate unique showmanship. They need to inform and educate the audience while also entertaining them. You can't do all that without intending to give and do your best.

3. Be Thankful and Grateful: *Speak with a Grateful and Thankful Heart*

I am so grateful and thankful I experienced an important "Aha" moment when I was younger. I watched a speaker deliver a presentation, and I saw him deliver with an attitude of gratefulness and thankfulness in his heart. Let me share with you the story through this illustration.

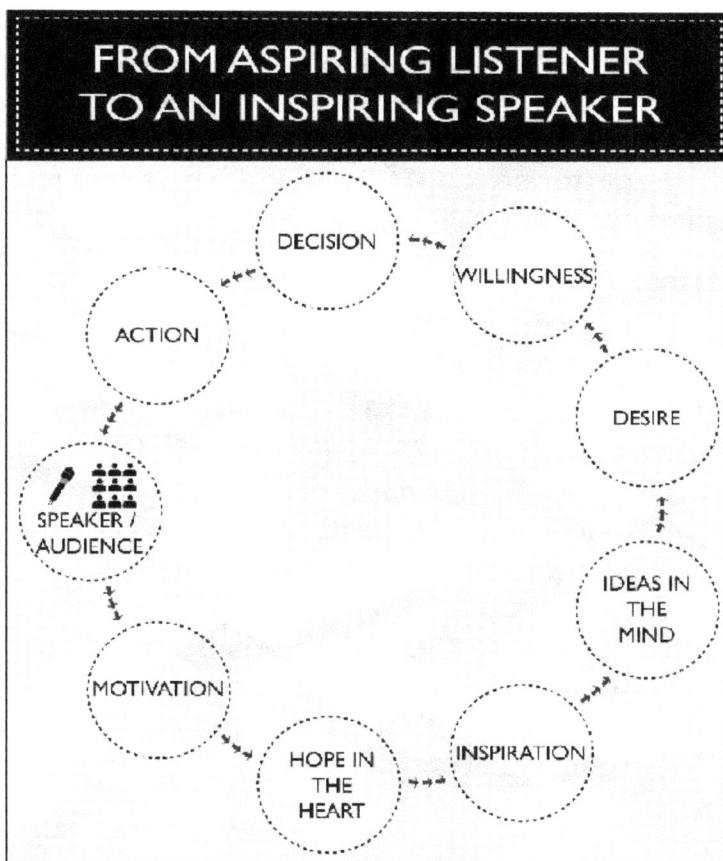

FROM ASPIRING LISTENER TO AN INSPIRING SPEAKER

Over two decades ago, I was just a part of the **audience**, aspiring to be inspired, and boy, was I inspired! I felt the **motivation** and **hope in my heart** that one day I could be a person who inspires others too, who is very confident in sharing her thoughts and ideas authentically.

I was so **inspired** that **ideas** overflowed in my mind; these ideas, in turn, birthed the **desire** and pushed my **willingness** into a big **decision**. *"I have to do something different." "I have to take **action**." "I have to be a professional speaker like him."*

As I heard the voice in my head, I got scared. But the cycle was not meant to be broken. I had to face the fear. I had to jump out of my comfort zone.

Today, I am grateful and thankful that even though the road I have traveled has not been easy, it gives me the direction to focus on my intention, which is to inspire my audience to also aspire to be speakers themselves.

For a life and business coach like me, one of the motivations that drives me to speak up is knowing I have the opportunity to inspire others too, the way that speaker from decades ago inspired me.

4. Stay in Faith

Faith diminishes worries.
A speaker who has faith in his audience
Attracts their full attention and cooperation,
Solidifies the message of the speaker,
And builds up to make a new and strong idea to the audience.

No speaker has perfect experience on stage all the time. They are built and strengthened by what they have learned from imperfect situations. Successful professional speakers have learned the art of staying in faith. I believe that if you are faithful to why you do and for whom you do what you do, even in the midst of imperfection, you will not entertain the destructive feeling called worry.

In unexpected situations, use your fear and mistakes to bring you to the next level of your speaking profession.

Remember the *3Ps* when you start doubting your speaking abilities: *Practice*, *Perform*, and *Progress* on a continuous basis.

Practice doesn't happen just during the few minutes you are on stage; it happens in the hours and days spent preparing, rehearsing, and refining. When you are practicing, it would be helpful not to do it alone. Seek feedback and suggestions. As I coach, even I need to be coached by others.

Perform to encourage and inspire. Don't perform for the sake of achievement or adulation. Perform using delivery techniques that help drive your audience to absorb, appreciate, and apply your message.

Progress to challenge your skills and your abilities. Your progress will define your abilities to move you to practice better, perform beyond expectation, and progress to higher and higher levels.

ﭤ *Brilliant Quick Tip* ﭜ

*Practice, progress, and perform on
a continuous basis.*

The *3Ps* will push you to get started and to move on to endless possibilities. It is unlimited indeed. You move on from someone who only wants to speak out to be heard, to someone who can be instrumental in positively changing the lives of your audience.

Your *3Ps*, your message, and *you*—your message on stage to your audience is actually your message to yourself too.

Speak Up and Lead

Speakers speak.
Speakers lead.
Leaders speak.
So . . . speak up and lead!

Most of the time, our ideas and leadership collect dust in our minds because we don't speak up. I remember my high school graduation day; I got truly inspired by all the speakers on stage.

I told myself I wanted to be like them. I liked the way they expressed themselves, the way they delivered their speeches, and the way they connected with people, especially the way they connected with me.

The desire in my heart was to improve my speaking skills. The willingness cultivated my dream to one day being able to effectively communicate with people even if just in a small group. But there was the matter of fear. The fear infected my reality—the reality that I haven't done it before. The fear often overpowered the desire, and so I just shut up and let the ideas rot in my brain.

But all that has changed.

How about you? How would you like to get started? What is the fastest way to turbo-charge your growth as a speaker?

If you have a message in your heart, start working, start believing, start speaking.

Start: *A Dozen More Good Tips*

Based on my own speaker journey, here are twelve tips for you to get started:

1. Decide to do it . . .whatever it takes.

2. Learn from the best speakers. Learn not only how they speak, but discover why they are passionate about what they do.

3. Start speaking. Everyone starts somewhere. Know your baseline level of skill and have a strategy to develop from there. Don't worry about making mistakes along the way. Every successful speaker has a history of mistakes that they actually used as jumping points for learning and improving.

4. Seek help; work with a coach. Have a thinking partner who can listen to you.

5. Practice. Practice. Practice.

6. Develop your content. Don't work only on your delivery, or else you will just be a shallow, noisy shell. Develop your competence. Internalize your profession.

7. Wage a war against clutter: organize, reorganize, and systematize. Set aside an hour a day for developing your speaking skills.

8. Be a purpose-driven speaker. Identify the purpose of your speaking; is it to motivate, to inspire, to challenge

your audience to take action? Then let your purpose drive the speech writing and delivery.

9. Define your niche and your goals as a speaker. Do you want to be a professional highly-paid speaker? Do you want a regular gig? Do you prefer to be a corporate speaker/facilitator? Or would you rather be an events and celebration host? Be clear about your goals.

10. Take care of your personal brand. Create your own distinct template. Update yourself by being aware of the current events in the community, city, or country of your audiences. Remain consistent to your brand image.

11. Get comfortable with your own skin.

12. Lastly, *focus* . . .

> ⋛ Focus on your goal, not on what people will think of you.

> ⋛ Focus on adding value.

> ⋛ Focus on the four principles.

> ⋛ Focus on being focused.

The Journey Continues!

My journey as a speaker is now being echoed by my experience in my new passion—body building. I'm a beginner again, and yet, what I'm learning from this experience, I can also apply to my public speaking career.

After my first international figure competition, I discovered that I cannot justify to the audience why I made some mistakes.

As a body builder/physique athlete and as a professional speaker, I have to remind myself before a show that my best friend and worse enemy is myself. As such:

1. I need to be prepared.

2. Materials, tools, and showmanship are needed.

3. The content of my mind must be crystal clear.

4. Confidence will come from my preparedness.

5. My voice will eventually get stronger.

6. Body movement can't be faked if you know you can't do something.

To further challenge your talents and abilities, here's a chart (on the next page) that you may use on a regular basis. Photo copy this chart and update it every year.

At Present You Know You Can Do	You Want to Accomplish in the Future	You Think Seems Impossible to Accomplish

What Makes a Speaker?

There are many different kinds of speakers. Here's the practical way to determine what kind of speaker you want to become. It's important to have a specific description.

- ≷ Be aware of which industry you are comfortable to speak about.

- ≷ Evaluate where your confidence comes from.

- ≷ Have a regular self-assessment for you to know what areas in your profession you need to work on.

- ≷ Be open to self-improvement. There are a number   of organizations that can help you organize your thoughts (based on your passion) and help you hone your skills. For me, it is Toastmasters International and The John Maxwell Team. Joining a Toastmasters club has been instrumental in my growth as a professional speaker. Look up Toastmasters on the web, and find a club close to you.

- ≷ Be willing to address your weaknesses. Learn from the experts. Take the necessary classes. Consciously and conscientiously correct problem areas.

- ≷ Have a clear understanding of where you get your motivation to speak; it will help you to be consistent in your message to your audience.

I thought I would remain as an aspiring audience forever, but I got inspired by the speaker who I enjoyed watching because he did his best, and I am thankful and grateful for the experience and for my faith that kept me steadfast in pursuing my goal of someday becoming an inspiring speaker. I did it!

And you can too. As you end reading this book, you may start moving to the next level of your career. I wish you all the best!

"True strength is the inner courage in pursuing what seems to be impossible."

~Coach Clarissa Calingasan

About Clarissa Gatdula-Calingasan

Clarissa Calingasan is a Filipino-Canadian certified life and business coach, author, teacher, entrepreneur, natural physique athlete, and speaker.

She is one of the founding partners of a highly prestigious group, The John Maxwell Team (JMT). She coaches/teaches the JMT Youth Max leadership program and also the young entrepreneurs of the Canadian Youth Business Foundation (CYBF) in Manitoba, Canada.

In the Philippines, she's been awarded the Outstanding Filipino Achiever Award (2012-2013) for her exceptional achievements in the business and the industry. Mentored by one of the world's famous philosophers, Bob Proctor, she co-authored with him the book entitled *The Magic of Winning.*

She founded Kaarawan Mo, Buhay Ko Foundation (Your Birthday, My Life Foundation), to help less fortunate children. She is a lifter and inspiration to many.

Learn more about Clarissa Gatdula-Calingasan at: CoachClarissa.com

Conclusion:
Become a ⋛Brilliant Speaker⋚
by Margo DeGange

Nothing can stop you from fulfilling that *thing* that's in your heart and that calls you each and every day, and if it involves speaking from the stage, you have the tools you need right here to get going with finesse and courage. You can be a master at what you are called to do!

It doesn't matter all that much if you are just starting out as a speaker, or if you have been doing it for years and simply picked up this book to help perfect your craft; all of us can benefit from the wisdom of others; all of us can use more advanced tools; all of us can increase in confidence; and all of us can be better equipped to care about the world and to reach others from the platform, using our God-given gifts.

You are a star, and you are already brilliant! I don't mean that flippantly or lightly. Your life is far more valuable than you may ever realize, and the impact you can have in this world, and in the lives of so many other people, is positively tremendous. Your voice is your greatest gift. I hope and pray you will use it with great wisdom and love. I believe you will.

Thank you for picking up this book. Thank you for reading it and seeing its value. Thank you for learning about some of the same topics from the vantage point of a variety of authors, and considering how they differ or why they are similar in their thinking—and why that is significant. Thank you for opening up to brand new ideas from some of them as well. Thank you for acknowledging the absolute and undeniable attributes of a brilliant speaker that many of these mentors agree upon and felt compelled to share, and thank you for respecting what they saw differently from one another, and why.

You have what it takes, you do. Never forget that. I've known people who couldn't walk the way most of us walk, or talk the way many of us can, or who don't look as attractive as the majority of us do. I've seen people take the stage with deep and widespread scars, unbelievable disabilities, enormous obstacles, and histories of gigantic hurdles and unbearable pain, and *that right there* is their triumph; they chose to inspire others through their stories and through their lives, using what they have, what they know, and what they have personally experienced.

If you *don't* want an excuse, you will never find one. That is what I believe in my heart for you: no excuses. Do what you came to planet Earth to do. Be who you know you are, and be eager and excited about that.

Create influence. Love your audience. Address their concerns. Instill in them the agreement that they *can* change their lives in positive ways, and give them the keys to begin to do just that—as soon as they go home.

I expect great things from you. We all do. I hope you will focus your speaking career on both *people and outcomes.* Influence the landscape. Help make the needed changes. Your small "corner" of the world, added to my small corner, added to all of our corners, makes a huge difference.

Desirable outcomes, that's what *brilliant speaking* is all about, and *you* get to be a part of it. Choose your pleasure; what will it be?

Will you—the *keynote speaker*—get everyone warmed up and prepared for the conference theme and the marvelous events ahead? Will you—the *after-dinner speaker*—loosen up the crowd and help them to wind down from the previous rigorous training sessions? Will you—the *breakout session speaker*—help attendees take needed action with clear tools and techniques they can put to use immediately following the training? Will you—the *seminar leader*—help transfer valuable skills to increase interpersonal communication in family life or in the workplace? Or, will you—the *general session speaker*—get everyone on the same page and inspired to follow the vision and mission set before them?

Your possibilities await you. The stars glisten with the hope that you take the tools you discovered here, and craft a meaningful message that's spoken from the heart. Then, apply the secrets you've learned in this book to get your message to the right people in the right way.

Are you ready *now* to become a brilliant speaker? You should be—it's your time! Get ready, get set, go for it! Take what you've received and bring it to the masses as you sparkle, shimmer, illuminate others, and shine!

With Great Love and Deepest Respect,

Margo DeGange

Splendor Publishing

Splendor Publishing

Books by Experts, to Help & Heal the World!

Splendor Publishing's life-changing books are written from the heart by skilled and passionate leaders, entrepreneurs, speakers, and experts with a mission to make a positive impact in the lives of others.

Splendor books inspire and encourage personal, professional, and spiritual growth. For information about our book titles, authors, or publishing process, or for wholesale ordering for conferences, seminars, events, or training, visit SplendorPublishing.com.

Further Training, Resources, and Personal Mentoring, Just for Speaker and Authors

If you want to learn more about becoming a brilliant speaker or a celebrated author, we can help. If you need personal attention and some assistance with the details that matter most to *you*—for your specific needs, we want to be on your team! We can help you as much or as little as you need, with the important things, such as:

✓ Crafting your message
✓ Defining your area of expertise
✓ Creating your speeches
✓ Writing your stories
✓ Outlining your manuscript
✓ Editing you work
✓ Publishing your book
✓ Marketing yourself as a Speaker and Author

Or, if you are a bit of a do-it-yourselfer, and you want to gain advanced, marketable skills to increase your influence, impact, discoverability, and reach, we have a number of solid and exciting programs suited for you, such as our:

⋛ *Book Brilliance Intensive*

⋛ *Speaking Brilliance Intensive*

⋛ *Personal Mentoring Program,* with
   Master Facilitator and Success Mentor,
   Margo DeGange, M.Ed.

Contact Splendor Publishing for more details at 979-777-2229.

www.ingramcontent.com/pod-product-compliance
Lightning Source LLC
Chambersburg PA
CBHW072115270326
41931CB00010B/1565